EAST AND WEST GERMANY: A MODUS VIVENDI

East and West Germany
A modus vivendi

KARL E. BIRNBAUM

SAXON HOUSE | LEXINGTON BOOKS

Published by

SAXON HOUSE, D. C. Heath Ltd.
Westmead, Farnborough, Hants, England

Jointly with

LEXINGTON BOOKS, D. C. Heath & Co.
Lexington, Mass. U.S.A.

ISBN 0 347 0101 5 6
LOC No. 73 1749
Printed in The Netherlands by D. Reidel Book Manufacturers, Dordrecht

Contents

List of Abbreviations

CDU/CSU   Christlich Demokratische Union/Christlich Soziale Union (Christian Democrats and their Bavarian wing, the Christian Social Union)

CMEA   (East European) Council for Mutual Economic Aid

CPSU   Communist Party of the Soviet Union

CSCE   Conference on Security and Co-operation in Europe

EEC   (West) European Economic Community

FDP   Freie Demokratische Partei (Free Democrats)

FRG   Federal Republic of Germany

GDR   German Democratic Republic

MBFR   Mutual Balanced Force Reductions

NATO   North Atlantic Treaty Organisation

SALT   Strategic Arms Limitation Talks

SED   Sozialistische Einheitspartei Deutschlands (Socialist Unity Party of Germany)

SPD   Sozialdemokratische Partei Deutschlands (Social Democrats)

UN   United Nations

USSR   Union of Soviet Socialist Republics

WTO   Warsaw Treaty Organisation

Preface

This book is a study of the accommodation in Central Europe achieved through the agreements of 1970–72. It is a sequel to my *Peace in Europe*, published in 1970 by Oxford University Press. The conclusions of the previous investigation, which I still consider valid, were marked by the tragic events of 1968 in Czechoslovakia that brought the emerging European *détente* to a standstill. The present volume attempts to analyse the policies that, only a few years later, produced the codification of a *modus vivendi* in Central Europe. In the concluding chapter I have tried to identify the conditions under which closer intra-European co-operation may develop across the ideological borderline that continues to divide the Old Continent.

Most of the research for this book was undertaken in my new capacity as researcher at the Swedish Institute of International Affairs, a position which I took up after having resigned from the directorship of the Institute in 1970. Early drafts of Chapters 1 to 3 were critically scrutinised by the research staff of the Institute in private meetings and seminars. A number of useful suggestions emerged from these discussions. I very much appreciated the excellent service rendered by the librarians of the Institute in locating and acquiring the source material for this study.

While the analysis is mainly based on available printed sources, the assessment of some crucial aspects of the negotiations and their results has been greatly helped by exchanges with persons directly or indirectly involved in the political processes which I have investigated. My sincere thanks are due to these busy officials and particularly to Egon Bahr for taking the time to talk and write to me at several instances during 1971–72 in the midst of pressing assignments of major political importance.

I owe a special debt of gratitude to Jacques Freymond, director of the Graduate Institute of International Studies, Geneva, who invited me to deliver three lectures on East-West relations in Europe at the Institute in May 1971. He thereby created an important incentive, which started me off on this project. It was completed in the late autumn of 1972, again at the Geneva Institute, whose teaching staff I had then joined at Jacques Freymond's invitation.

I have benefited a great deal from lecturing on subjects related to the main theme of this book at special meetings of scholars working at the *Institut für Internationale Beziehungen*, Potsdam-Babelsberg, in June 1971 and at the Institute for Advanced Studies, Princeton, in March 1972. I am grateful to Gerhard Hahn and Carl Kaysen, the directors of the two institutes, for arranging these meetings.

Early versions of Chapters 1 and 3 were presented at review sessions organised in March 1972 by Zbigniew Brzezinski and Marshall Shulman of Columbia University, New York, and by Robert Bowie and Stanley Hoffmann of the Center for International Affairs, Harvard University. I am indebted to them and to all those who, by participating actively in these sessions, helped me to eliminate mistakes and to discover new aspects of the problems under investigation.

Several persons have read and commented on parts or the whole of the manuscript at a more advanced stage in my work. Egon Bahr, Melvin Croan, Thomas Hart, George Kennan, Karol Lapter, Peter Ludz, Åke Sparring, Wolfgang Wagner and – last but not least – my father Immanuel Birnbaum have all, each in his own way, contributed to improving the end result, for which, of course, I alone bear the responsibility.

A final word of gratitude is due to my family and especially to my wife Britta, who again had to endure the hardships of life with a book-writing husband and father. I can only hope that the relief each time the ordeal is over is not the only compensation.

K. E. B.
Geneva, Christmas 1972

Introduction

Since the mid-1960s East-West relations in Europe have on the whole been moving in the direction of *rapprochement* and closer co-operation. Retrospectively, the tragic events of 1968 appear as a temporary set-back in this secular trend rather than its reversal. This is not to suggest that the repercussions of the Czechoslovak crisis will not be felt for a long time to come: clearly, the intervention of the Soviet Union and four other Warsaw Pact countries changed some of the basic premises for the relations between East and West in Europe. Yet, the early 1970s were again characterised by attempts to overcome the division of Europe at least in terms of an intensification of contacts and negotiations across the East-West borderline.

By mid-1972 a significant change could be registered. In the spring of that year Bonn's renunciation-of-force treaties of 1970 with Moscow and Warsaw were ratified, the Berlin accord concluded between the United States, USSR, Britain and France in 1971 came into force, and a first Soviet-American agreement was signed on the limitation of strategic arms. These acts, the outcome of lengthy negotiations, not only symbolised a distinct improvement of the international atmosphere: they also seemed to create the prerequisites for a qualitatively new East-West relationship.

What were the driving forces behind this transformation? And what were the potentialities of the new situation emerging in Europe? Two complementary approaches commend themselves for the study of these problems. The first implies an analysis of the patterns of recent and conceivable future interaction in East-West relations and thus of the scope for structural changes in the European sub-system of the international system. It involves scrutinising trends and options in trade, co-production, technological co-operation, migration, tourism, and other transaction flows between Eastern and Western Europe. The other approach concentrates on the official policies of the main actors and tries to ascertain priorities and operational goals of ruling elites in East and West. In the present study the latter approach has been used. A careful investigation of official policy would seem to be a necessary stage in any serious effort to understand and explain the behaviour of the main actors on the international scene.

In the realm of recent East-West relations the crucial role of ruling elites in bringing about a more congenial political climate and a trend toward a new overall situation has been particularly striking. Indeed, it can be demonstrated that some clearly identifiable initiatives on the part of individual governments produced the necessary preconditions for subsequent agreement and thus, ultimately, for the East-West package deal of 1970–71. In so far as this deal may well usher in a new period in the history of Europe, it appears justified to assess the implications and potentialities of the latest phase in East-West relations on the basis of a scrutiny of official policies leading up to that accord and following from it.

The focus of the present study on the policies of Moscow, Bonn and East Berlin has, of course, implied a narrowing of the scope of this investigation. It has meant that some of the major political processes impinging on the present and future situation in Europe could only be hinted at. The most important of these developments are the following: 1) the relations between the two super-powers, which may promote *détente* in Europe or conversely reach a point where the effort to safeguard the *modus vivendi* in Europe could be seriously endangered; 2) the relations of Western Europe with the United States, which are of the utmost importance for the outcome of East-West negotiations, since they involve the character and credibility of America's commitment to the defence of Western Europe, any change in which may influence the perceptions of the main actors on the European scene; the co-operation within 3) the Western European family of nations, and 4) within the socialist community of Eastern Europe, neither of which can fail to affect the future relations between the two parts of Europe. It can be argued, however, that the subject matter of this study, the western policy of the Soviet Union, Bonn's *Deutschlandpolitik* and the predicament of the GDR are the most dynamic and closely interrelated areas of policy immediately affecting conditions in the heart of Europe. Thus, there may be a case for concentrating on these highly interdependent aspects of European politics as long as the wider international framework is not lost sight of completely.

But if the ultimate purpose of the present study is to map out the potentialities emerging in Europe as a result of the East-West accommodation arrived at through the negotiations of 1970–72, the question arises: potentialities for what? At this stage the values and preferences of the author should be explicitly spelled out in order to give the reader a clear indication of his vantage point. Mine is the one of a person raised by a German family in Eastern and Northern Europe during the thirties and forties in a tradition of abhorrence of all forms of totalitarianism and sympathy for the ideas, if not always the practical policies, of West European social democracy. From this background and the study of contemporary international politics developed a natural preoccupation with the search for peaceful accommodation among nations, and particularly for *rapprochement* between East and West in Europe. At the present juncture of East-West relations the restoration of some form of unity within a pan-European framework would seem both necessary and possible.

In view of the global problems confronting mankind and the human and material resources available in Europe, the ultimate purpose of efforts to unify the Old Continent should not be confined to the elimination of threats to the security, independence and well-being of the European nations alone. While these will remain primary concerns, they must be combined with joint European ventures at the service of mankind as a whole, and specifically those underprivileged people, in both industrialised and underdeveloped countries, constituting its vast majority.

1 Normalisation of Soviet-West German Relations

It is generally recognised that Soviet policy in Europe since early 1969 has been marked by a distinctly conciliatory attitude toward the West and at the same time by determined efforts to consolidate Moscow's predominance in Eastern Europe. It is less evident what these developments signify with regard to the operational goals of Soviet policy in Europe[1]. Some observers in the West have asked themselves whether the new attitude means a shift in the perceptions of Soviet policy-makers and a corresponding reassessment of Moscow's priorities in Europe[2]; others have reaffirmed their conviction that the basic Soviet goals in Europe remain unaltered and that all we are witnessing at present is a change of tactics.[3] While the author belongs to the first rather than the second group, it would seem that speculation of this kind tends to support a widespread, but somewhat unrealistic, notion of the process of policy-making in the Soviet Union, and indeed in most societies with powerful bureaucracies. Those who have studied these processes generally agree that single decisions creating major new departures are extremely rare. As a rule shifts in the direction of policy occur as an incremental process, certain initial steps being taken with a view to opening up new options without giving up any of the old ones. In these circumstances, policy analysis should concentrate on the question whether the dynamics of interaction in international affairs may eventually lead decision-makers in a given country to the point where they would have to give up some of their original options in order to be able to exercise new ones. A number of indications suggest that in the course of 1970–71 the Soviet leadership reached such a point on the Berlin issue.

An analysis of this kind presupposes some notion about Soviet perceptions. We shall therefore start by trying to set out what in the light of Soviet actions and pronouncements during the second part of the 1960s would seem to have been primary preoccupations of the Soviet leaders relating to Europe, both East and West, and how they viewed the interdependence of developments in both parts of Europe. In a following section we shall then analyse some authoritative Soviet declarations and moves during the period since 1969 in an attempt to assess their significance for Moscow's perceptions of current requirements and opportunities in Europe.

1 Soviet perceptions of the European scene: an interpretative survey[4]

Although during the 1960s China emerged as a major contender to both super-powers, Soviet foreign policy remained Europe-centred. This was largely due to the Soviet contention that, in spite of the growing importance of developments in South East Asia and the Pacific, conditions in Western Europe will for some time continue to determine the basic power structure in the world, specifically the relations between the United States and the USSR. Thus, Western Europe, in Soviet eyes, appeared to constitute both a potential buffer-zone against the United States and a hostage to ensure good behaviour from the Americans. At the same time the West European capitalist societies, primarily West Germany, were perceived by the Soviet leadership as a challenge to the territorial status quo in Eastern Europe and to Moscow's dominant position in that area. But at least since the mid-1960s these same West European societies were also viewed as major sources of technological innovation and investment capital and thus as potential partners in joint economic, technological and scientific ventures. The overriding Soviet interest in Western Europe during the postwar years had been to prevent a closely knit transatlantic combination that could hold the preponderance of power on the European continent. This concern seems at times to have induced Moscow to develop contacts and co-operation with economically and technologically advanced capitalist countries in Western Europe, not only for the sake of the inherent mutual advantage but also as instruments for the purpose of fragmenting the Western alliance.

The single most important country in Western Europe from the Soviet point of view was undoubtedly the Federal Republic of Germany. This was so because West Germany appeared as the major stronghold of the United States on the European continent. American-West German relations in the economic, military and political fields were therefore conceived as the crucial link between America and Western Europe – the 'ignominious axis Washington-Bonn' as it used to be called in more polemical Soviet pronouncements of the 1960s. In addition, the very emergence and development of the West German state had been depicted in official Soviet policy statements as a challenge to the status quo in Central and Eastern Europe. It is one of the fundamental ambiguities of Soviet postwar policy in Europe, whether this official view was due to the specific policies conducted by consecutive governments of the Federal Republic or to the very character of West German society, or both. In any case, it is worth emphasising that in its dealings with Bonn, Moscow always retained sufficient leeway to keep open the option of a major deal with a non-communist West German government. This double approach to the Federal Republic – as a major challenge and a potential partner – probably reflected the fact that West Germany was recognised by the Soviet leaders not only as economically and technologically the most powerful state in Western Europe, but also as a country which, for a number of reasons, was highly susceptible to Soviet influence.

These perceptions produced a policy directed primarily at containing West German influence in Eastern Europe and at the same time retaining some Soviet leverage in West German affairs. Generally speaking, Moscow attempted to influence conditions in Western Europe in accordance with its preferences mainly by the following means:

a) threatening and, alternatively, conciliatory initiatives with regard to Berlin and other issues relating to the future of Germany;

b) the exploitation of intra-Western differences or rivalries, both between individual West European states and between Western Europe and the United States; and

c) concerted actions of indigenous Communist parties and other so-called 'peace-loving forces', specifically those in France and Italy.

As for Eastern Europe, the Soviet leadership appeared to see its relations with the heterogeneous group of countries belonging to the Warsaw Treaty Organisation from at least three major viewpoints. First and foremost, it saw these states as constituting a strategic zone of utmost importance to Soviet security interests. Secondly, they were seen as semi-autonomous partners in a common socio-economic system and in an ideological movement. Thirdly, it seems that Eastern Europe was considered by Moscow an important transmission belt for influencing the outside world, especially Western Europe.

From these perceptions have stemmed related ideas about the conditions in the East European countries compatible with basic Soviet interests. Thus, the Soviet leadership was anxious to acquire or retain reliable means of physical and political control in these countries, which usually meant some form of military presence and/or political leverage within each individual East European state. In addition, Moscow sought to promote economic and technological co-operation as well as ideological conformity within its East European sphere of influence, both as an end in itself and a means of protecting and further consolidating Soviet predominance in the area. Finally, Eastern Europe's function as a transmission belt required the closest possible co-ordination of foreign policy between Moscow and its East European allies. The main instruments for achieving these goals were the power of the Red Army, brought to bear within the framework of closer co-operation in the WTO, 'socialist division of labour' within CMEA, the manipulation of the West German threat, and varying degrees of dependence of the ruling East European elites on support from Moscow.

2 The reactivation of Soviet policy towards the West

All through the *détente* of the late 1960s the Soviet leadership was apparently well aware of the intricate interaction of developments in Eastern and Western Europe. The growth of contact and exchange between East and West afforded

3

Moscow an opportunity to achieve greater leverage in Western Europe, but at the same time exposed its own sphere of influence to the erosive impact of Western ideas. In that situation the Soviet leaders exerted themselves to make inroads in the Western part of the continent without jeopardising their control over its Eastern part. This involved allowing more interaction between East and West Europe with a view to loosening intra-Western ties and co-operation and at the same time improving economic conditions in Eastern Europe, which in turn could contribute to the consolidation of Communist regimes there. But the Soviet leadership was also anxious to hedge against political repercussions of this growth in East-West contacts, since it feared ideological contagion and greater autonomy of East European ruling elites. In the years 1967–68 Moscow therefore adopted a selective *détente* posture *vis-à-vis* Western Europe, which implied singling out West Germany, allegedly dominated by revanchist and militarist forces, as the great obstacle to peace and security in Europe. At the same time, the Soviet leadership argued that an effective exploitation of the opportunities opening up in Western Europe presupposed strengthening the unity of the socialist camp.[5] Events in Czechoslovakia during 1968 led to the collapse of this policy: the invasion revealed how much more the Soviet leaders cared about their firm control over Eastern Europe than about *détente* with Western Europe. But once 'consolidation' in Czechoslovakia had reached a certain point, Moscow could again afford to adopt a *détente* posture towards Western Europe.

By early 1969 a number of domestic and international circumstances seemed to call for a Soviet return to a more conciliatory attitude *vis-à-vis* the West. At home, declining economic growth rates were a cause of concern to the governing group in Moscow requiring *inter alia* improvements in labour productivity and the speedier introduction of new technology. A major shift of productive capacities to growth-oriented sectors of the economy, on the other hand, conflicted with what seemed to be two firm commitments of the Brezhnev/Kosygin leadership in its overall allocation of economic resources: to increase the output of consumer goods and to strengthen the military power of the Soviet Union.[6] In this situation, the expansion of trade and economic co-operation with the West, including long-term loans in Western currencies, offered some prospect for alleviating these internal pressures. This in turn, however, presupposed *détente* with the West.

On the international scene the Soviet Union, as a consequence of its action in Czechoslovakia, was faced with a reversal of the trend towards fragmentation in the Western alliance prevalent during preceding years. This trend had been due not only to the specific policies conducted by President de Gaulle but also to a more general feeling of transatlantic alienation caused in part by the war in Vietnam. The possibility of terminating membership of NATO as of 1969 had added a special dimension to the lingering crisis in the West.

But after August 1968 a distinct inclination to strengthen the alliance had again made itself felt, and there was no longer any real concern or wish to exercise the '1969 option'.

Since Moscow had always been anxious to prevent the emergence of an American-West European combination that could confront the socialist states with superior power on the European continent, the Kremlin was liable to search for ways and means to halt developments that pointed in that direction. A *détente* posture was the most obvious, time-honoured measure to adopt. Finally, the events in Czechoslovakia had been a traumatic experience for the whole of Eastern Europe and the switch back to *détente* with the West could serve as a sign of normalisation within the WTO.

In the course of 1969 the domestic and international incentives for the Soviet leadership to seek some accommodation with the West became even more pronounced. The performance of the Soviet economy in that year showed signs of falling further below expectations suggesting that overall results would be even more disappointing than those of the preceding year. China's anti-Soviet militancy was highlighted during the Ussuri incidents in March 1969, while the new Republican administration in Washington seemed determined to shift the priorities of American foreign policy from Vietnam to the global rivalry with Moscow. These developments were liable to enhance Soviet interest in the pacification of its Western flank through an agreement with Bonn, which could at the same time open up new opportunities for co-operation with advanced Western societies. But it was only toward the end of the year that the possibility of this option began to materialise.

Moscow greeted the incoming Nixon administration with assurances of Soviet readiness to initiate a serious exchange of views on the limitation and subsequent reduction of offensive and defensive strategic weapons.[7] With France, high level talks were resumed when 'The Grand Commission' was reconvened early in January 1969. The Federal Republic during these months also received a number of indications of a Soviet wish to improve relations. At the time these overtures seemed primarily to signify a Soviet concern to overcome the negative repercussions of the invasion of Czechoslovakia. But the shift to a *détente* posture *vis-à-vis* the West encouraged the other East European countries to propose new initiatives for peace and co-operation in Europe, since such steps could enlarge their relative freedom of action.[8] When in mid-March 1969 the Warsaw Pact leaders met in Budapest, the deliberations resulted in an appeal marked by the conspicuous absence of any polemics.[9] The Budapest document renewed the earlier Warsaw Pact proposals for the convening of an all-European conference on security and co-operation, and it afforded Hungary, Romania and Poland an opportunity to pursue a more active policy of *rapprochement* towards the West European countries on a bilateral level. Using the conference proposal as a cover, the leaders in

Budapest, Bucharest and Warsaw attempted to reassert their specific national interests in the new atmosphere of decreasing tension. This was most dramatically manifested in a speech by the Polish leader Wladislaw Gomulka on 17 May 1969, in which he suggested the conclusion of a border agreement with the Federal Republic without simultaneously insisting on recognition of the GDR.[10]

In spite of these events, Soviet declarations during the spring of 1969 implied no major change in Moscow's stance. A Soviet statement issued in connection with the spring session of the NATO ministerial council used harsh language and contained the standard indictments of the United States and West Germany as well as the traditional list of 'requirements' – including a non-nuclear status for the FRG and the recognition of existing European frontiers – that had to be met in order to safeguard European security.[11] The same was largely true of the main document adopted by the international conference of communist and workers' parties in Moscow on 17 June 1969.[12]

During the following months, the Soviet leadership continued to feel its way *vis-à-vis* the West in a general attempt to mend bridges and regain ground that had been lost in 1968. In the process, and partly under the influence of contacts with some leading West German politicians[13], the Soviet government began to display greater interest in a *rapprochement* with the Federal Republic. This was reflected in the conciliatory tone of the Soviet reply in September 1969 to a West German memorandum proposing the resumption of the bilateral talks that had been discontinued at the height of the Czechoslovak crisis.

A clear sign of Moscow's preference for bilateral dealings with Bonn came only after the change of government in the Federal Republic and the subsequent modification of the West German stand on some of the main Central European issues.[14] This new departure in Soviet policy was endorsed at an extraordinary meeting of top party and government leaders of WTO member states in Moscow on 3 and 4 December 1969.[15]

In opening up the new path of *rapprochement* with the Federal Republic the Soviet leadership apparently wished to explore the implications of a policy option, which had seemed to commend itself on several occasions in the postwar period, most recently to Mr. Khrushchev in 1964. Three main concerns could be discerned in Soviet pronouncements and actions when this exploratory operation was initiated. Firstly, the leaders in Moscow seemed determined to keep those East European states in line that were inclined to use the excuse of bilateralism, in preparation of the proposed Conference on Security and Co-operation in Europe (CSCE), for enlarging their own contacts with the West. Above all this was true of Hungary, Romania and – as a consequence of a reversal in the stand previously adopted by Mr. Gomulka – Poland. Secondly, the Soviet leadership was anxious to sustain an orthodox

6

ideological conformism among Soviet citizens in the face of pluralistic tendencies the impact of which were likely to be enhanced by a new round of *détente* with the West. Thirdly, Moscow had to overcome the opposition of the East German leaders to the new overtures to West Germany.

The first of these preoccupations prompted the Soviet Union to re-emphasise the so-called 'Brezhnev doctrine'[16] and the importance of close military collaboration within the framework of the WTO. In addition, the West German bogey, though no longer as prominent as in previous Soviet declarations, was nevertheless kept alive.[17] Subsequently, as negotiations with the West German government got under way, Moscow took some new initiatives in order to accelerate integration into the CMEA, which implied closer Soviet control over the economies and also the political manoeuvres of the East European allies.[18] The second concern appears to have induced the leaders in the Kremlin to step up the campaign for implacability toward bourgeois ideology and for social disciplinarianism, thus giving new impetus to the repressive trend in Soviet intellectual life. As for the third concern, East Germany, the Soviet objective seemed to be to overcome outright, without, however, risking serious destabilisation of conditions in the GDR, any opposition from its political elite to a *détente* in East-West relations. At the Moscow conference in December 1969 the leaders of the GDR were induced to back down on their previous demand that bilateral negotiations between any Warsaw Pact state and Bonn must be preceded by full recognition of the GDR on the part of the FRG. The reaffirmation of the demand that 'all states establish equitable relations with the German Democratic Republic on the basis of international law'[19] clearly fell short of East German claims. An understanding seems to have been reached to the effect that talks with Bonn were to be subject to co-ordination within the framework of the Warsaw Treaty Organisation, which suggested some undefined East German influence on the further development of East-West contacts.[20] But this did not turn out to be a serious restraint on Moscow's freedom of action in its bilateral dealings with Bonn during 1970.

As the Soviet leaders were embarking on the negotiations with West Germany, the international position of the Soviet Union was relatively strong. Moscow had reinforced its military presence in Central Europe and unfolded a significantly increased naval power in the Mediterranean. Soviet political influence in the Middle East was growing, while the conflict with China seemed to be moving, at least temporarily, into a less acute phase. At the same time the opening of talks with the United States on the limitation of strategic armaments (SALT) was liable to enhance Soviet self-confidence, since it created a kind of institutional framework on the super-power level and thus established a visible, symbolic parity between Moscow and Washington. Domestically, the situation was far from satisfactory, as evinced *inter alia* by Mr. Brezhnev's critical remarks about the performance of the Soviet economy at a CPSU central committee meeting in December 1969.[21] Thus, the Soviet leaders could view negotations with the Federal Republic from a position of relative strength, and in so far as they foresaw the possibility of a major deal with Bonn it is plausible to assume that they were moved at least partly by economic incentives.

Before the end of the year confidential bilateral talks between West German and Soviet diplomats started in Moscow. The Soviet attitude during the first exploratory contacts suggests that, as a result of the new signals and the first foreign policy decisions of the Brandt government, especially its decision to sign the nuclear non-proliferation treaty, Moscow was inclined to undertake a fundamental review of Soviet-West German relations.[22] At the same time these initial exchanges revealed the depth of mutual suspicions, accumulated in the course of more than two decades of hostile confrontation in the heart of Europe.

Even when the talks became more intensive, after the arrival of Chancellor Brandt's *alter ego*, State Secretary Egon Bahr, in Moscow,[23] the Soviet attitude remained for some time exploratory and non-committal. Yet, the net result of three rounds of negotiations between Foreign Minister Gromyko and Mr. Bahr, from 30 January to 22 May 1970, was something akin to a basic Soviet reassesssment of the new West German government's Eastern policy.[24] In early February 1970 the Soviet Union and the Federal Republic concluded a commercial agreement providing for Soviet deliveries of natural gas and West German credits of over 1 billion DM to finance exports of pipes and other equipment to Russia. This deal undoubtedly reflected Moscow's growing interest in 'businesslike' co-operation with Bonn. Some aspects of the Brandt/Scheel government's *Ostpolitik*, notably the continued adherence to the long-term goal of German unity through self-determination, must have appeared to the Soviet leaders as being contrary to their own designs and preoccupations. But in the course of negotiations they seem to have concluded that there was sufficient scope for an agreement formalising the status quo in Central Europe, and thereby creating a new basis for future Soviet-West German relations, including the extension of 'mutually advantageous collaboration'.

3 The Moscow Treaty

The treaty signed by Premier Kosygin and Chancellor Brandt in Moscow on 12 August 1970 implied the codification of the overriding common interest of the Soviet Union and West Germany in the pacification of conditions in Central Europe. If one compares the wording of the Moscow treaty with the respective positions adopted by the two sides during the abortive negotiations in 1967–1968,[25] it becomes evident that the agreement involved significant concessions on both sides. Its central elements were on the one hand the Soviet acknowledgement of the Federal Republic as an equal and reliable partner in international politics, and on the other hand the West German formal acceptance of the existing political and territorial status quo in Central Europe.

The nature of these undertakings explains the pros and cons of the Moscow treaty in relation to the basic interests of the two contracting parties. Official spokesmen of the Federal Republic have emphasised the importance of the treaty as a starting point for a qualitative transformation of East-West relations in Europe, that is its potentially *dynamic* character. Soviet pronouncements on the other hand have stressed the *static* elements of the treaty, implied in the article establishing the inviolability of existing European frontiers (Article 3). Thus, one of the main positive aspects of the treaty as seen from the Soviet side would seem to be the fact that West Germany's formal acceptance of the territorial results of the Second World War significantly decreased the West German challenge to Soviet hegemony in Eastern Europe.[26] The Soviet leadership, no doubt, must have taken note of the West German official view of the treaty as a starting point for *rapprochement* between East and West in Europe. It is, however, conceivable that Moscow was confident of keeping such a process under more effective control than during previous periods of *détente*, since it had lately succeeded in reinforcing its control over Eastern Europe by different means, including new bilateral agreements with the individual East European states.[27]

The hopes for change in East-West relations associated with the Moscow treaty were often directed in official Soviet declarations, to the development of 'practical' collaboration between the USSR and the FRG.[28] This supports the view expressed above that one of the major incentives for the Soviet leadership, in embarking upon the line of policy symbolised by the treaty, was the prospect of enlarging economic, technological and scientific co-operation with Western Europe and especially the Federal Republic.

If a scaling down of West Germany's challenge to the status quo in Central and Eastern Europe and improved possibilities for economic and technological co-operation with Western Europe were the main *positive* aspects of the treaty as seen from the Soviet side, what were its major drawbacks? The principal West German negotiator, Mr. Bahr, has emphasised the importance of Moscow's unqualified renunciation of the threat or use of force against the Federal Republic implied in the treaty. This, in his view, was tantamount to an expression of Soviet confidence in the Federal Republic as a peace-loving state, a position contrary to most Soviet and East European descriptions of conditions in West Germany during the whole postwar period.[29]

9

The main Soviet 'concession' implied in the treaty would thus seem to have been the basic change in Moscow's official view of West Germany's foreign policy. This change had two aspects. The confidence in West Germany's peacefulness or at least in the prevalence of 'peace-loving' forces in the Federal Republic, circumscribed Soviet freedom of action in Western Europe in so far as it deprived Moscow of the basic argument used since 1945 for claiming a right to intervene in West German affairs. It is true that by 1970 Soviet *armed intervention* in West Germany to prevent undesirable developments in that country appeared most unlikely. Yet, *politically*, interventionist claims against West Germany had continued to be a basic element of Soviet policy in Europe throughout the 1960s, whether those claims were based on the victorious powers commitment to extinguishing German nazism and militarism, or on the so-called 'enemy state clause' in the UN Charter (Articles 53 and 107).

The other aspect of the implied Soviet confidence in West Germany's peacefulness was related to conditions in Eastern Europe. It amounted to the virtual elimination of the West German bogey from the East European scene and thus to the disappearance of a policy posture which Moscow had consistently used to counter West Germany's influence in that part of Europe. Again, one could point to the fact that the credibility of Soviet warnings against the threat emanating from West Germany was increasingly difficult to uphold in the face of contradictory evidence available to a growing number of East Europeans. Yet, the almost automatic Soviet recourse to the 'German menace' as an instrument of consolidation in Eastern Europe was demonstrated during the Czechoslovak crisis. In addition, alleged West German aggressiveness had played an important part in the ideological campaign within the Soviet Union to increase vigilance against imperialist designs allegedly aimed at the subversion of the socialist camp. It is worth noting that the Brandt government considered the elimination of the West German bogey an important precondition for closer ties between the Federal Republic and the East European states.[30]

This interpretation is supported by authoritative Soviet pronouncements in 1971. For example, Premier Kosygin was at pains to explain to visiting West German industrialists and businessmen that any significant expansion of trade and economic co-operation presupposed the creation of political trust.[31] The same theme was hinted at by the Soviet Party leader, Mr. Brezhnev, in his report to the 24th congress of the CPSU, when he warned against the risk of a new crisis of confidence in the policy of the Federal Republic should ratification of the Moscow treaty be delayed.[32]

While the Moscow treaty involved give and take on both sides, its essence, the formalisation of present conditions in Central Europe, served Soviet rather than West German interests. A fair balance of mutual concessions, therefore, presupposed a package deal including at least an explicit Soviet acceptance of the status quo in the only place where this implied more of a Western advantage: Berlin.

4 Berlin and Moscow's new 'Westpolitik'

The initiative for the latest round of Four Power negotiations on Berlin was taken by President Nixon, when, during a visit to West Berlin on 29 February 1969, he declared that the situation in Berlin was not satisfactory and ought to be regarded by everybody as a call to action. After a positive Soviet response in Foreign Minister Gromyko's speech before the Supreme Soviets on 10 July 1969 and thorough preparations during subsequent months, the Berlin discussions of the four wartime allies – the United States, the Soviet Union, the United Kingdom and France – opened on 26 March 1970, in the building formerly occupied by the Allied Control Council in West Berlin.[33] The pace of the Berlin talks, which for a while ran concurrently with the bilateral negotiations between Moscow and Bonn, was at first very slow, and it was only after the conclusion of the bilateral USSR-FRG agreement that they picked up some momentum. Yet, the very fact that Four Power discussions on Berlin were going on was of crucial importance for the success of the negotiations between Moscow and Bonn.

The situation in and around Berlin had not been the subject of formal negotiations between Moscow and Bonn, since questions pertaining to Berlin and Germany as a whole were considered the sole responsibility of the Four Powers. However, in the course of the Bahr-Gromyko talks the West German side had consistently emphasised that an agreement on Berlin must be part and parcel of an overall East-West understanding in Europe, since conditions in and around the former German capital constituted one of the major international friction points on the Old Continent. The initiation of the Four Power talks on Berlin in March 1970 was therefore seen by Bonn as a vital part of the common Western effort to bring about a better *modus vivendi* in Central Europe. The West German government argued that while there could be no legal connection between a bilateral Soviet-West German deal on the one hand and an agreement on Berlin on the other, a *political linkage* between the two was inherent in the objective situation: it was impossible to achieve the goals set out in the Moscow treaty, while leaving the highly explosive conditions in and around Berlin untouched.

All through the negotiations of 1970 this fundamental position of the West German government remained unchanged. The essentials of a satisfactory Berlin agreement and the time sequence envisaged by Bonn between such an agreement and the ratification of a Soviet-West German treaty were clearly set out in one of the six guiding principles adopted by the Federal

11

Cabinet on 7 June, 1970, for the final stage of the negotiations with Moscow. It read as follows:

> The position of the Federal Government on the Berlin question remains unchanged. We proceed on the premise that the Four Power negotiations will guarantee the close ties between the Federal Republic and West Berlin and the unobstructed access to West Berlin. Without such guarantees, a treaty on the renunciation of force cannot become effective (*wird ein Gewaltverzichtsvertrag nicht in Kraft gesetzt werden können*).[34]

Yet, it is worth noting that the stand adopted by Bonn on this issue in late July and purportedly communicated verbatim to Mr. Gromyko, was somewhat less stringent than subsequent West German pronouncements sometimes made it appear.[35] In fact, it was compatible with the idea of 'parallel procedures', advanced eventually by Moscow as the proper solution to this complicated problem. Thus the West German side was clearly anxious to avoid rigidity on the linkage issue,[36] a point which should be kept in mind as suggesting that the Soviet leadership may have felt it enjoyed considerable latitude on Berlin, when signing the treaty with Bonn.

Moscow never accepted the notion that the ratification of the treaty presupposed a mutually satisfactory East-West agreement on Berlin. But in the course of 1970–71 the Soviet position on this question was gradually modified: from *explicit rejection* of any kind of link, via its *tacit acknowledgement* to the ultimate enunciation of a *counter-linkage*, implying that the Berlin agreement would not come into force prior to the ratification of the Moscow treaty.

On the basis of available evidence it is impossible to establish conclusively the factors determining Soviet performance in the Four Power negotiations on Berlin. Yet, some of the main considerations that seem to have played a decisive role in the formulation of Moscow's policy can be inferred from its actions and declarations before, during and after these negotiations.

While there had been no major crisis in Berlin since the early 1960s, the Soviet Union had repeatedly used the exposed location of West Berlin in order to exert pressure on the Western powers and to exploit differences among them. The potential for generating or exacerbating international tension and influencing intra-Western relations through actions in Berlin had thus remained one of the main instruments of Soviet foreign policy. In addition, the potential Soviet threat against the security and viability of West Berlin had at times been conceived as a deterrent against the implementation of alleged Western designs to undermine Soviet predominance in Central and Eastern Europe, notably in the GDR. At the beginning of the 1970s, therefore, the Soviet leadership faced the basic question of whether it was prepared to have its freedom of action narrowed significantly in a central area of world politics with both global and regional significance.

Subsequent events have confirmed the view[37] that Moscow's inclination to strike a major deal with the West on Berlin was founded on two basic assumptions: firstly, that the global rivalry with the United States could be kept within manageable bounds; and secondly, that Western, and especially West German, postures challenging the stability of prevailing territorial and political conditions on the other side of the European dividing line were being reduced to a point where Moscow could afford to demobilise its counter-challenges in Berlin. Progress in Soviet-American talks on the limitation of strategic arms and developments in the Middle East were probably the major indicators of whether the first of these assumptions was justified. The second must necessarily have been influenced not only by Moscow's own interpretation of the modified West German stand, but also by its assessment of the situation in Eastern Europe, in particular the views of the most exposed among its allies, the East German leadership.

The Soviet Union had argued that the treaty with Bonn would facilitate an agreement on Berlin. If the above reasoning is largely correct, the Soviet contention was valid, since the Moscow treaty implied a solemn undertaking on the part of the Federal Republic to observe strict non- interference in the internal affairs of any state in the Soviet orbit. What remained unclear was whether the Soviet leaders would ultimately consider this de-escalation of the Western challenge to Soviet rule in Eastern Europe to be sufficient for them to reduce their leverage *vis-à-vis* the West in Berlin. The East German leaders did their utmost to prevent Moscow from coming to that conclusion. They persisted in bedevilling West German designs in Eastern Europe and continued to denounce any kind of West German political presence in West Berlin as an unbearable threat to the GDR and to the whole socialist camp. The Soviet leaders could not afford to disregard the expressed apprehensions of the SED, lest the latter's power – and ultimately the relative stability of conditions in East Germany – be undermined. On the other hand, they had to take into account the fact that Mr. Ulbricht and his associates were inclined to exploit their domestic weakness in order to induce the Soviet Union to adopt a policy which would not only help to secure the survival of the East German power elite – a common interest of Moscow and East Berlin – but also enhance its influence in the socialist camp.

In view of the stakes involved, it is hardly surprising that before seriously contemplating concessions the Soviet leaders should try to have their cake and eat it too, to avoid paying the price in Berlin for the new options that the treaty with Bonn seemed to open up. Soviet pronouncements and negotiating behaviour during the early autumn of 1970 suggest that Moscow wished to explore and if possible exploit two distinct possibilities: firstly, that the Brandt government, in view of its own domestic difficulties, might lose its

13

nerve and be susceptible to Soviet pressure to ratify the Moscow treaty without prior agreement on Berlin; and secondly, that Western unity with regard to the Berlin issue might falter, thus enabling Moscow to reap the benefits of its deal with Bonn and yet escape any, or at least any major, concessions in Berlin.

In September and early October 1970 the Soviet side displayed an adamant attitude in the Berlin negotiations, while at the same time demanding the rapid ratification of the Moscow treaty and rejecting the notion of any link between the two.[38] But by the end of October 1970 the Soviet leadership apparently had reached the conclusion that the Western allies were united on the essentials of a Berlin accord.[39] Furthermore, as a result of the Hesse elections in early November 1970, the outcome of which was more favourable to the FDP than expected, the domestic position of the Brandt/Scheel government had been consolidated. Hence, speculations about its susceptibility to pressure appeared increasingly unwarranted. Finally, it must by then have been clear to the Soviet leaders that whatever the mental set-up of Mr. Brandt and his associates, the necessary majority in the *Bundestag* would simply not be forthcoming, unless there was a tangible prospect for an agreement on Berlin that the Federal Government could present as 'satisfactory'. Since the Brezhnev/Kosygin leadership displayed a marked determination to pursue the policy-course embarked upon with the signature of the Moscow treaty[40], the Soviet Government was apparently induced to reconsider its tactics. During the latter part of autumn 1970 a number of signs indicated that Moscow was beginning to put some pressure on the East German leaders to adopt a more conciliatory attitude in order to enlarge its own freedom of manoeuvre in the Four Power negotiations on Berlin. The Soviet position was supported by the Polish Government, whose negotiations with Bonn were successfully concluded in mid November 1970 with the initialling of a treaty on the normalisation of relations with the FRG[41], the final validation of which, however, was also dependent on a satisfactory Berlin agreement.

The efforts to co-ordinate WTO positions on Berlin reached a first culminating point at the meeting of Warsaw Pact leaders in East Berlin on 2 December 1970. This conference formulated some of the criteria for a Berlin agreement in terms that were hardly to the full liking of Mr. Ulbricht and his associates.[42] Shortly afterwards, however, Moscow's Western policy temporarily lost its momentum as a result of the popular uprising along the Polish Baltic coast at the end of the year, which led to the fall of the Gomulka regime. Since these events were liable to wake Soviet apprehensions of similar eruptions elsewhere in Eastern Europe, they tended to strengthen the position of the GDR leadership *vis-à-vis* Moscow and also the influence of those forces in the Soviet power elite who, mainly for reasons of domestic discipline, opposed a policy of *détente* with the West. Consequently, the beginning of 1971 was marked by some confusion in Moscow about the direction of its policy towards the West.

This period of uncertainty lasted until about the middle of February 1971. By then the unrest in Poland had been largely contained, and the new leadership under Edward Gierek seemed to be able to consolidate its position, partly by significant concessions to consumer demands. Similar steps, clearly dictated by the Polish experiences, had been announced in East Germany in connection with the 15th Plenary Session of the SED Central Committee at the end of January. From the Soviet side came contradictory signals during the early weeks of 1971, suggesting an internal controversy within the ruling elite: on the one hand hints of disenchantment with the Brandt government and of a slackening of interest in a Berlin agreement and the ratification of the Moscow and Warsaw treaties; on the other hand assurances that the Soviet leaders recognised the importance of a Berlin accord for *détente* in Europe, and wished to elicit early ratification of the treaties.[43] But on 13 February 1971, the main line of Moscow's Western policy was reaffirmed in an authoritative article in *Pravda*, which emphasised that 'the treaties ... reflect the balance of interests of the parties' and that 'treaties in the interests of peace cannot give one of the participants more and the other less ...'.[44] While the article did not mention Berlin, its reasoning implied that it was unjustified to couple the ratification of the treaties with a Berlin agreement. But the *absence of any explicit rejection* of the connection with Berlin in this article and also in the communiqué from a WTO meeting of Foreign Ministers in Bucharest on 18–19 February 1971, suggests that Moscow was now inclined tacitly to accept it.[45]

The main speeches delivered at the 24th Congress of the CPSU clearly demonstrated the prevalence of the political forces favouring an agreement with the Western powers on Berlin as an essential element of East-West *détente*.[46] The Soviet stand with regard to the relationship between ratification of the treaties and a Berlin accord was clarified in so far as Mr. Gromyko explicitly called for 'parallel procedures'.[47] This seemed compatible with the official West German position, if it was understood that a substantive agreement in the Four Power talks must be achieved before the ratification process could be initiated.

A breakthrough in the Berlin talks occurred in May 1971, and at their meeting on the 28th of that month the four ambassadors were able to produce jointly a skeleton agreement as the basis for final negotiations.[48] This progress was made possible by the fact that the Soviet Union, reversing its previous stand that East Germany as a sovereign state had an unlimited right to control civilian traffic to West Berlin, declared itself ready to assume responsibility for the unimpeded civilian transit traffic through the GDR between the Federal Republic and West Berlin. While the considerations leading to Moscow's change of attitude and to subsequent Soviet concessions, cannot be established conclusively three developments would seem to have been of decisive importance in this connection:

1) the departure of Walter Ulbricht from the leading post of the SED in early May 1971 and the ensuing reshuffle in the East German governing group;

2) the Soviet-American consensus announced on 20 May 1971 with regard to the scope and nature of an agreement limiting the strategic armaments of the two super-powers;

3) the growing indications during spring 1971 of an impending American-Chinese *rapprochement* culminating in the announcement on 15 July 1971 of President Nixon's visit to Peking.

The change of leadership in East Germany enabled Moscow to elicit from the SED its explicit consent to the kind of concessions deemed necessary for a final agreement with the West on Berlin.[49] The preliminary accord in the SALT reflected the mutual interest of the super-powers in avoiding an unlimited arms competition.[50] It was liable to inspire the Soviet government with increased confidence that global rivalry with Washington could be managed without recourse to the mechanism of crisis generation in Berlin. Finally, the American-Chinese *rapprochement* enhanced the powerful incentives, domestic as well as international, which seemed to be pushing the Soviet leaders in the direction of a major deal with the West in Europe.[51]

The quadripartite agreement on Berlin signed on 3 September 1971 implied a formalisation of the realities that had evolved there in the course of the postwar period. Some aspects of these, notably the close ties between the Federal Republic and West Berlin, had become a matter of considerable concern to Moscow, mainly because of the unfavourable repercussions on the stability of East Germany. By formally acknowledging the existence of these ties and by consenting to their further development[52] the Soviet government made a major concession to the West. It was made possible by the fact that the agreement also implied a reciprocal scaling down of aspirations challenging prevailing conditions on the other side of the Wall. Indeed, one of the most significant features of the Berlin agreement was that neither side could credibly retain their traditional concepts of the threat that Berlin offered to their security, be it the idea of a Western bridgehead in the midst of communist dominated territory as an instrument to achieve German reunification on Western terms, or the opposite (Eastern) goal of eliminating the Western enclave by frontal assault or 'salami' tactics. Both sides accepted a situation whose abnormality could henceforth become an incentive for steps towards normalisation rather than a reason for undermining the stability of social and political structures on the other side.

The validation of the Berlin accord had been made dependent on inter-German agreements regulating the civilian traffic between the FRG and West Berlin as well as the access of West Berliners to East Berlin and the GDR. Available evidence makes it reasonable to assume that Mr. Brezhnev intervened personally in East Berlin at the end of October 1971 in order to speed up these negotiations. Shortly before Christmas 1971 the agreements complementing the Four Power accord were signed between representatives of the Federal Republic and West Berlin on the one hand and East Germany on the other.[53] While these agreements did not satisfy all expectations on the West German side, they were considered sufficient for the Brandt government to initiate the process of ratifying the Moscow and Warsaw treaties.

In the meantime Moscow had begun to show a renewed sensitivity to procedures and had expressed concern lest the West German *Bundestag* withhold ratification of the treaties in spite of major Soviet concessions in Berlin.[54] By the time of West German Foreign Minister Scheel's visit to Moscow at the end of November 1971 it had become clear that the Soviet government insisted on a 'counter-linkage', implying that it would not sign the final protocol of the Berlin agreement until the ratification process in the West German parliament was concluded.[55]

The decision to adopt this adamant position – which, however, was in full accord with the concept of 'parallel procedures' announced at the 24th Party Congress by Mr. Gromyko – seems to have been the result of a careful calculation on the part of the Soviet government of the stakes and risks involved in the final stages of a major deal with the Western powers.[56] The Brezhnev/Kosygin leadership had committed itself to a policy aimed both at consolidating the status quo in Europe and at making it possible for closer co-operation with the advanced West European countries. It had encountered and, to all appearances, overcome considerable opposition to this line of policy within the CPSU itself. But in view of the long years of enmity towards the FRG and the vested interest of some powerful elements in the Soviet bureaucratic apparatus in retaining that policy posture, it can be assumed with some confidence that the proposed change of policy towards West Germany continued to be a contested issue in leading party circles. While Mr. Brezhnev and his closest associates had attempted to complement the changed attitude towards the FRG by closer relations with other states in the West, notably France[57], the treaty with Bonn was the heart of the overall concept. If, due to political developments in the Federal Republic, the agreement with West Germany failed to materialise, this would invalidate the basic premises of the foreign policy conducted by the governing group since 1969. Such a set-back, in turn, could well threaten its political survival, especially if it had committed itself to a stand which implied major concessions in Berlin prior to the formal fulfilment of Western undertakings.

If these were the Soviet perceptions of the stakes and risks involved in the final stage of the package deal with the West, it is hardly surprising that Moscow decided to establish a 'counter-linkage' in order to guard against unfavourable contingencies.[58]

This prudence on the part of the Soviet leaders was justified by events in the course of spring 1972. Since the Brandt government's parliamentary majority in the *Bundestag* was being steadily eroded, the outlook for West German ratification of the Moscow and Warsaw treaties appeared by March 1972 most uncertain. In this situation the Soviet side displayed concern about the polarisation of political forces in the FRG and sounded notice on the West German public that non-ratification would imply a major set-back in East-West relations. These stern warnings were clearly meant to dispel any hopes that the CDU/CSU leaders might have had of re-negotiating the Eastern treaties.[59]

At the same time the Soviet leadership exerted itself to promote the West German ratification process. Two types of measures were instituted by Moscow for this purpose: on the one hand steps aiming at a systematic refutation of the main objections adduced by the CDU/CSU against Bonn's Eastern treaties; on the other hand efforts to demonstrate the advantages that would accrue to the FRG from the implementation of the deal.

Among the first type of measures can be mentioned the decision to incorporate in the Soviet ratification process 'the letter on German Unity' handed over by Mr. Scheel to Mr. Gromyko on the occasion of the signing of the Moscow treaty.[60] This implied that Moscow took official cognisance of this document, a gesture which tended to invalidate the contention of the CDU/CSU that the Soviet-West German treaty precluded any future striving for German unity through self-determination. In addition, Mr. Brezhnev, in a speech on 20 March 1972, acknowledged the existence of the European Community in terms that suggested an inclination to come to terms with this important grouping of states on the basis of a mutual recognition of the organisational frameworks for economic co-operation in Eastern and Western Europe.[61] That stand was liable to weaken another of the arguments of the West German opposition, namely that the Moscow treaty and the policy based on it would lead to an erosion of West European integration.

The improvement of conditions in divided Berlin was foremost among the advantages that West Germany derived from the deal with Moscow once it had been validated.[62] Thus, when in early April 1972 representatives of the Soviet Union and the Federal Republic initialled an agreement on trade and economic co-operation, West Berlin was explicitly included in it.[63] While this was in accord with the Four Power agreement, the fact that Moscow put these stipulations on paper before the Berlin arrangements had come into force tended to underline Soviet willingness to ease conditions in Berlin. The same was true of the announcement that a Soviet delegation would participate in the Federal Congress of West German trade unions to be held in West Berlin in June 1972.[64] The demonstrative Soviet acceptance of the ties between West Germany and West Berlin, implied in the holding of this meeting at the proposed place, was clearly meant to show that Moscow was determined to include Berlin in the European *détente*, once the package deal had become valid.

5 Soviet policy in Europe: perspectives after the East–West package deal

What were Soviet assessments of the perspectives opening up after the satisfactory conclusion of East-West negotiations? And what did authoritative pronouncements suggest about evolving expectations and goals among Soviet policy-makers? Writing in the immediate aftermath of the Crimean meeting between Leonid Brezhnev and Willy Brandt, which took place in mid-September 1971 shortly after the Berlin agreement had been signed, *Pravda's* chief foreign policy commentator, Yury Zhukov, expressed the following view:

> We are approaching in Europe the boundary between two stages – the post war stage, which was characterised by the atmosphere of the 'cold war' and the arms race, and a new stage, the stage of all-European businesslike co-operation ....[65]

The steps envisaged by Zhukov for passing from one stage to the other included not only the validation of the main elements of the East-West package deal but also preparations for an all-European conference and an agreement on the reduction of armed forces and armaments in Europe. He concluded by asserting that the implementation of the proposed measures would have a beneficial effect on bilateral USSR-FRG relations and, in particular, create opportunities for the substantial expansion of businesslike co-operation in all fields, including the economic.[66] As was to be expected, these perspectives were in full agreement with the comprehensive peace programme elaborated in the Central Committee report to the 24th CSPU Congress in the spring of 1971.[67]

During 1971-72 two main themes dominated official and semi-official Soviet statements dealing with current European affairs: firstly, the improvement of bilateral relations with individual West European states, notably the FRG and France; and secondly, the urgent need to convene an all-European conference to tackle the problems of security and co-operation (CSCE).

Ever since the reactivation of its Western policy in 1969, the USSR had sought to cultivate its ties with Paris. These efforts became of special importance in a period of dramatically improved relations with West Germany.

The Soviet leadership was apparently anxious to avoid giving the impression that the signature of the Moscow treaty implied a preference for the Federal Republic as the USSR's major partner in Western Europe. In Soviet accounts of the main international developments during 1970–71 the 'new stages' attained in relations with France and West Germany were usually presented as of equal significance.[68] This stand, as well as the renewed campaign to convene an all-European conference, indicated a Soviet wish to retain some leverage in Western Europe as well as a concern for the negative repercussions of accelerating West European integration where the interests of the East European states and the cohesion of the Soviet alliance were concerned.[69]

However, the CSCE proposal clearly served as a multi-purpose device in Soviet diplomacy. The Warsaw Pact states had eventually consented to North American participation in an all-European conference, but Soviet spokesmen did not cease to depict the policy of the United States as one of the main obstacles to peace and security on the Old Continent. Arguments adduced by American officials against the *early* convocation of the CSCE were repeatedly adduced as evidence of the alleged fundamental incompatibility between European and American interests.[70] The clash between Western Europe and America on trade issues and the concomitant monetary crisis in the Western world were registered as proof of the correctness of these Soviet assessments. In this situation Moscow presented the CSCE as a safe way for the West Europeans to escape from the humiliations, frustrations and uncertainties accruing from their association with America.[71]

If the exploitation and furtherance of transatlantic alienation was the main purpose behind the Soviet *campaign* for an all-European conference, the advantages expected from the actual *preparation* for the conference would primarily seem to have been related to consolidation in Eastern Europe. It is worth noting that, when in late June 1970 the foreign ministers of the Warsaw Treaty states proposed to initiate *multilateral* forms of preparing the conference[72], Moscow had, by and large, concluded its bilateral negotiations with the Federal Republic and was exerting itself to bring the East European allies in line.[73] This suggests that, having witnessed how individual states in Eastern Europe had used the bilateral preparation of the all-European meeting as an excuse for enlarging their contacts with the West, and being for its own part very close to a major deal with the Federal Republic, the Soviet leadership was anxious to pass on to *multilateral* negotiations in preparation for the conference in order to be able to control more effectively the Warsaw Pact policies towards the West.

The foregoing is not meant to imply that the Soviet Union had no genuine interest in the convocation of the CSCE. The purpose is rather to show that policy makers in Moscow derived different benefits from the *campaign* for, the *preparation* for, and the actual *holding* of that conference.

What, then, could the Soviet leadership plausibly hope to achieve as a consequence of one or several conferences on security and co-operation in Europe? Since the holding of a CSCE was unthinkable without the participation of the GDR on equal terms with other states, the very involvement of the GDR in an all-European diplomatic setting was in itself apt to stabilise further the East German state and its government. The Moscow and Warsaw treaties of 1970 had implied a *bilateral* formalisation of the territorial and political situation in Central Europe between the parties most immediately affected. Beyond this, however, Moscow was also anxious to secure the *multilateral* recognition of prevailing conditions in Europe, as shown by its repeated pleadings in favour of East German membership of the UN, which presupposed the consent of the Western powers. The convening of the CSCE would be an important step in that direction. On the basis of this consolidated position Moscow apparently wished to extend economic and technological co-operation with Western states and to negotiate with them about the reduction of forces and armaments in Central Europe.

Our analysis would seem to confirm the findings of other Western observers, that what the leaders in Moscow mainly hoped to achieve with the package deal of 1970–71 was, firstly, the formalisation of the status quo in Europe, thus consolidating Soviet predominance in its Eastern part, and secondly, the development of close technological, scientific and economic collaboration with Western Europe. Both these goals can, in turn, be explained in terms of a search for ways of reallocating political attention and material resources at a time when world politics seemed to focus on developments in Asia and when the improvement of living standards among the broad masses of the USSR had been proclaimed by the party leadership priority number one.[74]

What has not generally been recognised, however, is the interdependence of the two goals in Soviet perceptions, and particularly the fact that East Germany, due to its geographical position, economic strength and residual political instability, constituted a crucial link between them. Soviet declarations and actions over the last few years permit the conclusion that the consolidation of the GDR as a member of the socialist community and as an equal European state was viewed by Moscow as a necessary precondition for the desired extension of East-West trade and collaboration. Ultimately, therefore, the Soviet leaders' hopes of realising their plans in Europe hinged on the question of *whether the relations between the two German states could evolve in a fashion that would allow an opening towards the West without jeopardising either the short term stability or the long term viability of a communist regime in East Germany.* It is to the policies of the two German states that we must turn in order to gain a better understanding of the potentialities arising from the pacification of the European scene through the package deal of 1970–71.

Notes

1 For a stimulating analysis see Richard Löwenthal, 'Continuity and Change in Soviet Foreign Policy' *Survival*, Jan-Feb. 1972, p. 2ff.

2 See, for example, V. V. Aspaturian, 'Soviet Aims in Eastern Europe' *Current History*, Oct. 1970, pp. 206ff.

3 Cf. interview with Malcolm Mackintosh in *US News and World Report*, 2 Nov. 1970, reprinted in *Survival*, Jan. 1971, pp. 27f.

4 This section is mainly based on the findings contained in the following works: Adam B. Ulam *Expansion and coexistence: the history of Soviet foreign policy 1917–1967*, London 1968; Thomas W. Wolfe *Soviet Power and Europe 1945–1970*, Baltimore and London 1970; Karl E. Birnbaum *Peace in Europe: East West Relations 1966–1968 and the Prospects for a European Settlement*, London, Oxford and New York 1970.

5 Cf. Leonid Brezhnev's speech at the Karlovy Vary conference in April 1967, *Information Bulletin* 8 (Peace and Socialism Publishers, Prague 1967) p. 35.

6 Cf. Wolfe, *op. cit.* p. 245f.

7 See Soviet government declaration of 20 January 1969, *Soviet News* no. 5473, 21 Jan. 1969, published by the press department of the Soviet Embassy in London.

8 For a discussion of Hungary's and Romania's plea for reviving the forces of *détente* see my *Peace in Europe*, pp. 98–100.

9 *Soviet News* no. 5481, 18 March 1969. For evidence suggesting that the wording of the Budapest appeal was a result of a compromise within the Warsaw Pact. see A. Ross Johnson, 'The Warsaw Pact's Campaign for European Security' *Rand Report*, November 1970, pp. 21–23.

10 See Gomulka's speech at Warsaw, 17 May 1969, *Daily News* (Warsaw) 18 May 1969. According to unconfirmed reports Gomulka's initiative was undertaken without notification of Moscow.

11 See *Tass* statement of 9 April 1969.

12 *Soviet News* no. 5495, 20 June 1969.

13 Prominent leaders of the FDP and SPD visited Moscow during summer 1969, among them Messrs. Walter Scheel and Helmut Schmidt, who only a few months later became respectively Foreign Minister and Defence Minister in the new West German government.

14 The changes in the West German position are discussed in Chapter 2.

15 Cf. A. Ross Johnson, *op. cit.*, p. 27.

[16] The so-called Brezhnev doctrine of state sovereignty being subordinated to the principles of socialist internationalism was reconfirmed in the joint Soviet-Czechoslovak statement signed on 27 October 1969 at the end of an official visit of Czechoslovak leaders in Moscow (*Soviet News* no. 5515, 4 November 1969). A document that had been drafted during the Warsaw Pact foreign ministers' meeting in Prague on 30–31 October 1969 proposed that a pan-European treaty on the renunciation of force would not invalidate previous international agreements. This could imply that 'fraternal assistance' among socialist countries on the Czechoslovak model of 1968 to defend 'socialist achievements' would not be contrary to the proposed treaty. See *Europa-Archiv* 4/1970, p. D90.

[17] The communiqué after the meeting of the Warsaw pact leaders in Moscow on 3–4 December 1969 registered a number of positive tendencies in the Federal Republic after the change of government in Bonn. Yet, it again called for vigilance against 'the unceasing dangerous manifestations of revanchism and the reactivation of neo-nazi forces in the Federal Republic of Germany ...' (*Soviet News*, no. 5520, 9 December 1969).

[18] See Summary of Communiqué from the 24th session of CMEA in *Soviet News* no. 5543, 19 May 1970, and announcement about the setting up of an international investment bank of CMEA on 10 July 1970 in *Soviet News* no. 5551, 14 July 1970.

[19] *Soviet News*, no. 5520, 9 December 1969, p. 118.

[20] Cf. Karl E. Birnbaum, 'Västtysk östpolitik efter maktskiftet', *Världspolitikens dagsfrågor* 4/1970, p. 14.

[21] A summary of what was presented as an 'unusually candid report' by Leonid Brezhnev, exposing shortcomings of the Soviet economy at a Central Committee meeting in mid-December 1969, was published in *Pravda* 13 January 1970.

[22] This seems to be borne out by the fact that in the course of three meetings in December 1969 the Soviet delegation was anxious to elicit from the West German side a basic declaration about the goals of West Germany's policy *vis-à-vis* the Eastern powers. See Carl-Werner Sanne, 'Zur Vorgeschichte des Vertrages', in *Der Vertrag vom 12. August 1970 zwischen der Bundesrepublik Deutschland und der Union der Sozialistischen Sowjetrepubliken* (published by the Press and Information Office of the Federal Government), p. 80. (Henceforth cited as *Der Vertrag*.)

[23] See Chapter 2, p. 38

[24] On the basis of available evidence it is impossible to say exactly when Moscow became ready to strike a deal with Bonn. Mr. Bahr, in a conversation with the author on 12 December 1971, suggested that his meeting with Premier Kosygin on 13 February 1970 was an important turning point.

[25] The documents exchanged in the course of the confidential Soviet-West

German contacts 1967–68 were published at the height of the Czechoslovak crisis in July 1968. For a full documentation see *Europa Archiv* 23/1968, pp. D362ff.

[26] Cf. leading article in *Pravda* 13 August 1970.

[27] For the text of the new Soviet-Czechoslovak treaty of friendship, co-operation and mutual assistance signed on 6 May 1970, see *Soviet News*, no. 5542, 12 May 1970. While the new Soviet-Romanian treaty, signed on 7 July 1970, contained no reference to the principles of limited sovereignty, the conclusion of the treaty was hailed by Premier Kosygin as an important expression of the desire to consolidate the international solidarity of socialist states and as a rebuff to the opponents of socialism attempting to drive a wedge into the socialist community. Cf. speech by Alexei Kosygin in Bucharest in connection with the signing of the Soviet-Romanian treaty, *Soviet News* no. 5551, 14 July 1970. On 13 August a protocol was signed on co-ordinating the plans for the development of the national economies of the Soviet Union and the GDR for the period 1971–75 (see *Pravda*, 14 August 1970).

[28] See, for example, the speech by Premier Kosygin during the official luncheon for Willy Brandt at the Kremlin on 12 August 1970, *Pravda* and *Izvestiia*, 13 August 1970.

[29] See Egon Bahr, 'Der Vertrag mit der Sowjetunion', in *Der Vertrag* p. 65. The absolute nature of Moscow's renunciation of any right to intervene unilaterally in West Germany is borne out by point 4 in the declaration of Foreign Minister Gromyko of 29 July 1970, which was subsequently agreed to be a constituent part of the USSR-FRG agreement. Gromyko's declaration was published when on 13 December 1971 the West German government initiated the process of ratification. Cf. *Bulletin* no. 186, 15 December 1971.

[30] See, for example, the government declaration in 'Gewaltverzicht und Zusammenarbeit', *Bulletin* no. 108, 14 August 1970; cf. also Karl Moersch, 'Kontinuität und Wandel der deutsch-sowjetischen Beziehungen sit 1949', in *Der Vertrag*, pp. 81ff.

[31] Cf. Hermann Pörzgen, 'Die Sowjetunion braucht den deutschen Handel nicht', *Frankfurter Allgemeine Zeitung*, 1 February 1971. See also J. Rubinsky, 'Logic of Coexistence. Problems of economic co-operation in Europe', where it is stressed that 'confidence between partners is the keystone of trade and all the more of long-term economic co-operation', *Izvestiia*, 26 December 1970.

[32] For Brezhnev's pronouncements before the 24th CPSU Congress on 30 March 1971, see *Pravda* 31 March 1971.

[33] For a short chronology of the origin and development of the Four Power negotiations on Berlin, see *Quadripartite Agreement on Berlin September 3*,

1971 (published by the Press and Information Office of the Federal Government), pp. 114ff.

34 See *Der Vertrag*, p. 155. The quotation in the text is taken from the official English translation of this publication entitled *The Treaty of August 12, 1970*, p. 139.

35 The relevant minute of the Cabinet resolution of 23 July 1970, which according to a West German government spokesman (cf. *Der Vertrag*, p. 67) was read *verbatim* to Mr. Gromyko by his German counterpart, Mr. Scheel, ran as follows (*ibid.*, p. 167):

> Die Bundesregierung ist der Auffassung dass Fortschritte in der europäischen Entspannung untrennbar verbunden sind mit Fortschritten in Richtung auf eine befriedigende Regelung der Lage in und um Berlin. Ein Gewaltverzichtsvertrag wird daher erst in Kraft gesetzt werden können, wenn entsprechende Vereinbarungen vorliegen.

This wording left open the interpretation that a Four Power agreement on Berlin *opening up prospects* for a satisfactory settlement would be sufficient precondition for *initiating* the process of ratifying the Moscow treaty on the West German side. In his paraphrase of the Cabinet decision of 23 July 1970 Mr. Conrad Ahlers, the government's press spokesman, used language that was hardly capable of that interpretation. See *ibid.*, p. 70.

36 Mr. Brandt repeatedly emphasised that he wished to avoid a strait-jacket for the procedures leading to the ratification of the treaties and a Berlin agreement. See, for example, his interview with *Südwestfunk* reproduced in *Süddeutsche Zeitung*, 12 October 1970.

37 Expressed by the author in a lecture on East-West relations, given before the Graduate Institute of International Studies, Geneva, 10 May 1971.

38 Cf. Gerhard Wettig, 'Betrachtungen zum gegenwärtigen Stand der Berlin-Frage', *Berichte des Bundesinstituts für Osteuropäische und Internationale Studien* 61/1970, pp. 18ff

39 This clearly was the message Foreign Minister Gromyko brought home from conversations with Western political leaders in early autumn 1970, and these impressions were apparently corroborated during President Pompidou's visit to the Soviet capital in October 1970.

40 As evinced *inter alia* in Mr. Brezhnev's speeches of 2 October and 29 November 1970 (*Soviet News*, nos 5563 and 5571, 6 October and 1 December 1970).

41 For the text of the Polish-West German agreement see *The Treaty between the Federal Republic of Germany and the People's Republic of Poland*, Press and Information Office of the Federal Government [Wiesbaden 1971].

42 See the communiqué from the WTO meeting in East Berlin on 2 December 1970, *Soviet News* no. 5572, 8 December 1970. Cf. also below, Chapter 3, p. 59

[43] See Richard Löwenthal, 'Kreml am Kreuzweg', *Die Zeit*, 19 February 1971, and statements made by the leading CDU politician, Gerhard Schröder (in the West German television programme 'Kontraste' on 21 January 1971) reporting on his conversations with Premier Kosygin and other Soviet leaders during a visit to Moscow. Cf. also Josef Riedmiller's report 'Das Abkommen bleibt, das Unbehagen auch' in *Süddeutsche Zeitung*, 10 February 1971.

[44] Unsigned article in *Pravda*, 13 February 1971, entitled 'When the interests of the peoples are ignored'.

[45] The communiqué from the Bucharest conference of Warsaw Pact foreign ministers contained an emphatic denunciation of the new link that the NATO ministers, at their meeting in Brussels in December 1970, had established between a Berlin agreement and the convening of a conference on security and co-operation in Europe. The absence of any explicit rejection of the connection with Berlin, however, was conspicuous. See *Soviet News* no. 5578, 23 February 1970.

[46] See report of the Central Committee of the CPSU to the 24th Congress, delivered by Leonid Brezhnev on 30 March 1971, *Pravda*, 31 March 1971; address by Foreign Minister Andrei Gromyko before the same forum on 3 April 1971, *Pravda*, 4 April 1971.

[47] *Ibid.*

[48] See *The Quadripartite Agreement on Berlin September 3, 1971*, Part II, 'Historical Background', p. 119.

[49] See Chapter 3 below.

[50] For the text of the Soviet-American announcement on SALT issued 20 May 1971, see *Soviet News* no. 5589, 25 May 1971.

[51] Richard Löwenthal has convincingly argued that the compulsions sensed by the Soviet leaders in 1971 left them little choice but to seek an accommodation with the West. See his article 'A World Adrift', *Encounter*, February 1972.

[52] Cf. *The Quadripartite Agreement on Berlin September 3, 1971*, p. 21.

[53] See Chapter 3 below.

[54] According to newspaper reports the Soviet Foreign Minister conveyed these concerns to his West German colleague during their meeting at the UN headquarters in New York, early October 1971. Cf. reports in *Süddeutsche Zeitung*, 8 and 9 October 1971.

[55] See Josef Riedmiller, 'Bei deutschem Wein die Frage der Fragen', *ibid.* 30 November 1971.

[56] Cf. leading article in *Pravda*, 4 September 1971, on the Berlin agreement; 'Big Stride towards Stronger Peace', English translation in *Soviet News* no. 5604, 7 September 1971.

[57] In autumn 1971 the Soviet Union engaged in a diplomatic offensive aimed at reasserting its influence in the socialist camp and the Third World as well

as at improving its relations with individual countries in the West. It included visits by the top Soviet leadership to Algeria, Canada, Cuba, Denmark, France, Yugoslavia, Morocco, North Vietnam, and Norway. Special importance was attributed to closer Soviet-French co-operation, which according to a leading article in *Pravda* on 1 November 1971 had 'entered a qualitatively new stage as a result of Leonid Brezhnev's visit to France'. For the joint Soviet-French communiqué and the agreed 'Principles of co-operation between the USSR and France', both issued on 30 October 1971, see *Soviet News* no. 5612, 2 November 1971.

[58] The Soviet concerns and the precautionary tactics to which they gave rise were reflected in repeated assertions to the effect that the Moscow treaty even *prior to its ratification* constituted a major political event of great international significance. See, for example, Brezhnev's speech at Baku on 2 October 1970, *Soviet News* no. 5563, 6 October 1970, and the communiqué issued on 18 September 1971 in connection with the meeting of Brezhnev and Brandt in the Crimea, *Soviet News* no. 5606, 21 September 1971.

[59] See Brezhnev's speech before the 15th Congress of Soviet Trade Unions on 20 March 1972, *Pravda*, 21 March 1972; for the English text cf. *Soviet News* no. 5632, 28 March 1972. See also Gromyko's address at a joint meeting of the foreign affairs committees of the Supreme Soviet on 12 April 1972, *Pravda* 13 April 1972, and President Podgorny's remarks on the occasion of Mr. Ulrich Sahm being accredited as West German ambassador to the Soviet Union on 26 April 1972, *Süddeutsche Zeitung*, 27 April 1972.

[60] See Chapter 2, p. 40. For the text of the 'Letter on German Unity', see *The Treaty of August 12, 1970*, p. 10.

[61] See *Pravda*, 21 March 1972. For an English translation cf. *Soviet News* no. 5632, 28 March 1972.

[62] For advantages in terms of inter-German normalisation see Chapter 3 below.

[63] For an official West German declaration announcing the initialling on 7 April 1972 of a long-term agreement on trade and co-operation between the FRG and the USSR see *Bulletin* no. 51, 11 April 1972, pp. 727 f.

[64] Cf. report by Josef Riedmiller in *Süddeutsche Zeitung*, 22 March 1972.

[65] Yury Zhukov, 'Programme of peace in action', *Pravda*, 23 September 1971.

[66] *Ibid.*

[67] Cf. Note 46.

[68] Thus the signature of the Soviet-French protocol of 13 October 1970 in connection with President Pompidou's visit to Moscow was usually represented as of equal value to the USSR-FRG treaty of 12 August 1970; see for example Brezhnev's speech at Erevan 29 November 1970, *Soviet News* no. 5571, 1 December 1970; also A. Gorokhov 'The USSR's struggle for European security, *International Affairs* (USSR) January 1971, and the resolution

adopted at the Plenary session of the Central Committee of the CPSU on 23 November 1971 on the international activities of the Central Committee after the 24th Party Congress, *Pravda* 24 November 1971.

[69] See K. Popov, 'West European integration and international co-operation', *Voprosy Ekonomiki* 1/1971. Cf. also A. Ross Johnson, *The Warsaw Pact's Campaign for 'European Security'* pp. 49 ff.

[70] See, for example, Boris Dmitriev, 'From a Europe of conflict to a Europe of lasting peace', *Pravda* 11 May 1971; also Spartak I. Beglov, 'Die aussenpolitische Plattform des XXIV. Parteitages der KPdSU', *Deutsche Aussenpolitik* 5/1971.

[71] Cf. Nikolai Kuznetsov, 'Knot of contradictions', *Pravda*, 18 November 1971.

[72] See memo of WTO foreign ministers approved at a meeting in Budapest 21–22 June 1970, *Soviet News* no. 5549, 30 June 1970.

[73] The Gromyko-Bahr negotiations were concluded on 22 May 1970. Cf. above p. 8.

[74] Cf. *24th Congress of the CPSU, March 30–April 9 1971, Documents* (Novossty Press Agency Publishing House, Moscow 1971) pp. 50 ff.

2 Bonn's Deutschlandpolitik under the Brandt/Scheel government

1 The legacies of the 1960s

Bonn's active Eastern policy initiated cautiously by Foreign Minister Gerhard Schröder in 1963–64 reached a new stage in late 1966 with the formation of the government of the Grand Coalition, which included representatives of the FRG's two major political parties, the CDU/CSU and the SPD. The new indications from the Kiesinger/Brandt government implied a major break with the legacies of the past. But the efforts to achieve reconciliation with the East were seriously hampered by differences between the coalition partners on the goals and means of West Germany's relations with the Eastern powers, differences that they barely managed to cover up by using the ambiguous concept of a 'European peace order' as the FRG's long term foreign policy objective.

Two overall concerns seem to have dominated the thinking of West German policy makers on foreign affairs at that juncture: firstly, the need to adapt to the general *détente* policy of the West, if Bonn were to avoid isolation within its own camp; and secondly, the necessity of breaking the deadlock in inter-German relations, lest the two parts of the German nation become increasingly alien to each other and the division of Germany and Europe be accepted as permanent.

On the first point the views of the CDU/CSU and the SPD were sufficiently close to each other to institute a major shift in West Germany's stand. It implied that *détente* and *rapprochement* between East and West were no longer conceived of only as consequences of progress toward German reunification but, in accordance with the prevailing Western view, as necessary preconditions for a development which could bring that ultimate goal within reach. On the second point (the deadlock in the relations between Bonn and East Berlin), however, the positions of the main partners in the Grand Coalition were far apart. The CDU and CSU based their policy on the expectation of continued hostility between the Soviet Union and the West and were sceptical of any plans that assumed a convergence of interests and priorities between Bonn and Moscow beyond that of avoiding war. As for East Berlin, they refused to contemplate a strategy that implied acceptance of a long term coexistence between two equal political regimes on German soil.

The Social Democrats, on the other hand, saw both Moscow and its East European allies, at least potentially, as genuine partners in a process of co-operation and mutual adaptation, which could open up the prospect of East-West reconciliation and of a lasting peace on the Old Continent. Consequently, the SPD leadership viewed the SED as an important counterpart to any future negotiations on the wider issues of security and co-operation in Europe, a counterpart, moreover, which had to be approached on the basis of full equality.

These fundamental differences made the West German *Ostpolitik* under the government of the Grand Coalition distinctly ambiguous. While Bonn, during the years 1966–68, asserted that its aim was to 'overcome' the division of Europe and of Germany, it was unable to clarify the implications of these long-range objectives. Subsequent developments, however, suggested that such clarification was absolutely necessary if Soviet mistrust of West German designs were to be alleviated and a start at least made toward *rapprochement*.[1] The lack of a clear-cut West German position on relations with the GDR enhanced the excessively fearful and defensive Soviet attitudes of those years, since the shift in Bonn's Eastern policy exacerbated Moscow's difficulties with its own allies, some of whom showed a distinct inclination to intensify contacts with the West. When in 1968 these tendencies, in combination with internal developments in Czechoslovakia, were perceived as a challenge to Moscow's rule over Eastern Europe, the Soviet leadership decided to intervene with armed force to safeguard its interests.

On balance, it could be argued that the change initiated by the Grand Coalition in the direction of West Germany's Eastern policy was successful in the sense that it managed to bring Bonn back into the mainstream of Western policy towards the East. At the same time, however, it contributed to developments in the Soviet sphere that led to a hardening of the division of Germany and Europe. When in October 1969 Willy Brandt formed a new West German government, based on the support of the SPD and the FDP, one of his main tasks in the field of foreign affairs was to make a new attempt at overcoming the complete impasse in inter-German relations. More than ever before, *Deutschlandpolitik* became the heart of Bonn's *Ostpolitik*.[2]

2 The basic policy concept

The origins of the basic concept determining the SPD/FDP government's Eastern policy can be traced back to the summer of 1963. On 15 July 1963, Egon Bahr, who was then press secretary and consultant to West Berlin's Mayor Willy Brandt, put forward some unorthodox ideas on relations with East Germany in a speech before the *Evangelische Akademie*, Tutzing. Bahr's reassessment was based on a close analysis of the Kennedy Administration's peace strategy and its repercussions on the situation in divided Germany.[3] The upshot of his argument was that, in view of the new global setting for East-West relations in Europe, the only realistic prospect for an improvement of conditions in Germany was by way of a gradual change through *rapprochement* between the FRG and East Germany. The traditional Western approach of 'all or nothing', of free elections or continued deadlock in the relations between the two parts of Germany, had to be substituted by a policy of small steps. This new policy must take into account the instability of the East German regime and the fundamental interest of the USSR in forestalling upheavals in East Germany. Bahr therefore suggested that Bonn might consider decreasing pressure on the East German regime, thus enabling the SED leaders to grant more opportunities for inter-German contact without undue fear of destablising conditions in East Germany.

At the time, these proposals were severely criticised by the whole political establishment of the FRG, including the SPD leadership. However, in the course of the 1960s it became increasingly clear that the central ideas in Bahr's concept were in line with prevailing international tendencies. Since West Germany's official policy during the latter part of the 1960s was largely dictated by the requirements of East-West *détente*, the formula *change through rapprochement*, coined by Bahr in his 1963 speech, came to appear as the most realistic prescription for an active Eastern policy in the Federal Republic. But it was only in 1969, with the formation of the Brandt/Scheel government, representing political forces which were in agreement on the major issues of West Germany's relations with the East, that these ideas could be made the basis of concrete policy measures. When, in late 1971, Mr Bahr summarised the main concept underlying West German *Ostpolitik* during the two preceding dramatic years of East-West negotiations, the continuity in his thinking since 1963 was striking.[4] Two fundamental assumptions were at the heart of his reasoning:

1) The recognition that German reunification through the accession of East Germany to the Federal Republic was most unlikely. Consequently the bringing together of the two parts of Germany was conceivable only as the result of a lengthy historical process.

2) The conviction that Moscow could not afford to risk any developments that, in its view, might jeopardise the viability of a communist regime in East Germany. In the last resort, therefore, Moscow would be determined to use force in order to assure the continued rule of the SED in the German Democratic Republic.

From these assumptions Mr Bahr deduced that for the foreseeable future the main objective of West Germany's Eastern policy must be the normalisation of relations between the FRG and the GDR. In his view, the GDR leadership had used its powers in the WTO to veto all measures aiming at *rapprochement* between East and West; therefore Bonn, in 1969, was faced with the task of removing this impediment, which could only be achieved by way of Moscow. Since the Soviet leadership had displayed a distinct interest in the formalisation of the status quo in Europe, the question arose of how far this Soviet interest could be used to promote measures that would make the division of Germany less inhumane; make the position of Berlin safer; and, in general halt or even reverse the growing alienation of the two German states.

The crucial problems confronting Bonn in the realm of *Deutschlandpolitik* were thus as far as possible approached by Bahr in terms of an adaptation of West German policy to the requirements and opportunities emerging from international developments, notably the attitudes and actions of the super-powers. In 1963 this above all implied keeping in line with American efforts to forge a new relationship with Moscow, based not only on a distinct determination to oppose Soviet expansion, but also on an acceptance of the status quo in Europe and a recognition of common super-power responsibilities for peace and stability in the world at large. At the end of the decade the most conspicuous trend was the change in Soviet attitudes, opening up opportunities for an improvement of East-West relations in Europe. But the new international setting of the 1970s also included an America interested in redefining its worldwide commitments, with, as a consequence, the prospect of its military presence on the European continent being reduced.

3   Domestic and international determinants of Bonn's 'Ostpolitik'

The significance and applicability of the Brandt government's basic policy concept can be properly assessed only in the light of an analysis of domestic and external constraints determining Bonn's scope and propensity for action.

The slender majority of the coalition partners, the SPD and the FDP, that had emerged as a result of the *Bundestag* elections in September 1969, might plausibly have led them to exercise caution and restraint where new departures in foreign policy were concerned, or to seek the greatest possible bipartisanship in the conduct of external affairs. Neither of these procedures was actually chosen, since other considerations seem to have prevailed in the governing group.

Both the SPD and the FDP were committed to the proposition that a reactivation of West German *Ostpolitik* under their leadership could open up new vistas in East-West relations. In view of this commitment, emphatically reasserted in the course of the election campaign, Messrs Brandt and Scheel were bound to take some major initiatives aiming at reconciliation with the East at the earliest possible moment.[5] They had reason to believe that a more comfortable majority of the electorate than the one reflected in parliament favoured an active Eastern policy along the lines they had proposed. However, the consolidation of this potential majority required that the new *Ostpolitik* produce some tangible results within the foreseeable future; and, since the new leadership in Bonn was convinced that their credibility *vis-à-vis* the Eastern states depended on their attitude to the positions held by the CDU/CSU on central issues of East-West relations, Chancellor Brandt and Foreign Minister Scheel had virtually no alternative but to dissociate themselves from some of the basic notions held by the opposition. Rather than compromise on these issues they chose to operate, rather daringly, on a narrow parliamentary majority, the precariousness of which largely determined the pace at which a reorientation of West Germany's policy towards the East – and specifically towards East Germany – could be instituted.[6] Yet, there had to be a perceptible change if a new start were to be made on the road to a better *modus vivendi* in Europe.

While the interdependence of domestic constraints and external opportunities was *one* important set of circumstances conditioning the direction and pace of Bonn's new *Deutschlandpolitik*, the interaction of the FRG's Western and Eastern policies constituted *the other* main determining factor. It was a basic tenet of Mr Brandt and his associates that the efforts to achieve some accommodation with the East could yield lasting results only on the basis of cohesion in the West and a close co-ordination of Western policies towards the East. This stand implied that solidarity between North America and Western Europe, as well as the furthering of West European integration, was thought a necessary precondition of reconciliation with the East. Consequently, the latter could never be sought at the expense of Western co-operation. The importance of this basic stance, which constituted an element of distinct continuity in West German foreign policy could only be enhanced by the fact that it had been emphasised right from the start by a government strongly committed to a more active and consistent Eastern policy than the one conducted by its predecessors.[7]

However, it was one thing to enunciate these lofty principles; it was a different, far more complicated matter to elaborate a definite programme of action fitting into the framework of a common Western strategy. The new West German leadership was clearly convinced that success in the attempts to dismantle the structure of confrontation in Europe initially required bilateral negotiations between Bonn and the Eastern states. Only the renunciation of claims previously upheld by the Federal Republic could credibly reassure the East, while West German fears were mainly focused on Soviet designs and capabilities. But however faulty and outdated the Rapallo syndrome must appear on closer examination, any spectacular bilateral arrangements between Bonn and Moscow were liable to arouse suspicion and concern among the Western allies, unless balanced by other steps. What made this West

German dilemma manageable was the possibility of achieving greater cohesion in the West, which emerged as a result of the reorientation of American foreign policy under the Nixon administration, and the departure of General de Gaulle from the international scene.

The new government in Washington seemed determined to move 'from confrontation to negotiation' and to free itself from the shackles of the unhappy involvement in Vietnam in order to regain greater freedom of action both at home and abroad. At an early stage the Republican administration had demonstrated that it accorded high priority to the revitalisation of America's relations with Western Europe chiefly through closer transatlantic consultation. But Washington had also indicated its willingness to leave ample scope to the West European allies in the management of intra-European affairs, including the exploration of any new opportunities for accommodation with the East.[8] In addition, the withdrawal of General de Gaulle from the political scene, by eliminating a major source of acrimony in American-French relations, had improved the prospects for a common Western approach to East-West relations in Europe. Indications from de Gaulle's successor, President Pompidou, also seemed to suggest that, after years of stagnation, some progress could again be made in the direction of further West European integration.

Thus, by the autumn of 1969 the prospects for balancing new ventures in the East with steps promoting consolidation in the West were comparatively promising. In this situation, bilateral initiatives on the part of Bonn were clearly in line both with the thrust of American policy and with the specific approach recommended and practised by France for many years. West German *Ostpolitik* could therefore be presented and justified as part of a wider Western effort to achieve accommodation with the East, though the interdependence of Western cohesion and East-West *détente* necessarily remained a source of constant concern to a government firmly committed to the promotion of both.[9]

4   The negotiations of 1970–71

The most important change in West Germany's *Ostpolitik*, announced at the very outset in the SPD/FDP government's first declaration of 28 October 1969, was the explicit acknowledgement of the German Democratic Republic as a separate state on German soil.[10] But Bonn still withheld diplomatic recognition from East Germany and declared that it would continue to do so on the ground that the GDR could not be treated as a foreign country: its people it was asserted, belonged to the same German nation as the inhabitants of the FRG and also the Four Victor Powers retained rights and responsibilities with regard to Germany as a whole. The Brandt/Scheel government refrained from adopting an all-embracing formula for its new policy towards the GDR, for to do so was thought to facilitate the task of those forces, both inside the FRG and abroad, who were liable to oppose the new West German stand. The shift in policy, therefore, was reflected not only in official declarations but also in the avoidance or more cautious use of previously employed terms (notably 'reunification') and in changed diplomatic practice. A step which was enunciated explicitly, however, was the partial elimination of West Germany's embargo against East Germany's international contacts. The reversal of Bonn's position on this issue was not complete, since it only applied to the *economic* and *cultural* fields; as for the *political* ties between the GDR and third countries, and also with regard to East German representation in international organisations, the new government in Bonn declared that its attitude would depend on the willingness of East Berlin to improve in a substantive and practical sense the relations between the two German states. This stand was accompanied with appeals to third countries not to interfere between them, by extending diplomatic recognition to the GDR, as long as there was a prospect of negotiations between the two German states, or, later, as long as negotiations were in progress.

This policy, however, suffered from ambiguity where Bonn's *ultimate* goals *vis-à-vis* the GDR were concerned. The emphasis which the West German side put on common nationhood and especially the connection established between progress in inter-German relations on the one hand and West German consent to the international recognition of the GDR by third countries on the other were apt to be resented and denounced by East Berlin. Indeed, this stand was later construed by East German spokesmen as evidence of a West German desire to dominate the GDR, blackmailing it into submission, and thus as proof of the prevalence of subversive designs against East Germany among the policy makers in Bonn.[11]

The attitude of the SED was predictable, and there is reason to believe that it was taken into account in the formulation of Bonn's new *Ostpolitik*. However, the position of the SPD/FDP government on the central issues of East-West relations in Europe should be assessed not only in terms of its expected effect in the East – important as this consideration was – but also as a necessary step in a process of domestic adaptation to the realities in Central Europe.[12] From the latter point of view relations with East Germany were one of the most sensitive areas of policy. The publicly proclaimed West German policy posture *vis-à-vis* the GDR can be properly understood only if one is aware of the domestic situation prevailing at that time in West Germany. Since there was a distinct element of taboo-breaking involved in the whole operation on which Mr Brandt was determined to embark, the process of change had to be gradual, lest escalating eruptions and subsequent set-backs were to result in a new impasse. The connection between substantive normalisation of FRG-GDR relations and West German acquiescence in the international recognition of the GDR by third countries should not, therefore, be viewed only as a bargaining device aimed at promoting a more co-operative attitude from the SED: the West German posture, later decried by the East German leaders as the so-called 'Scheel doctrine' must also be seen against the background of the very dynamics of the situation. No government in Bonn could disregard the fact that West German voters assessed the SED largely on the basis of what they learnt about the latter's performance in East Germany: the less repressive the policy of the GDR leaders, the greater the inclination of the public and government in the FRG to accept diplomatic recognition of the GDR by third states.

In view of these domestic constraints, it was essential for the success of Bonn's new Eastern ventures that *confidential* bilateral talks be initiated with each of the main partners in the Warsaw Pact, including the East German government. Only in this way could the West German leaders hope to eliminate old suspicions and lay the foundation for mutual confidence.

Like its predecessor's, the SPD/FDP government's Eastern policy operated on three levels: firstly, the Soviet Union; secondly, the East European states, with Poland this time in a key position; and thirdly, East Germany. A fundamental characteristic of West German negotiating procedures in the early 1970s was the unambiguous determination to accord first priority to relations with Moscow. As a consequence, Bonn took specific care to avoid any steps that could be construed as an attempt to undermine the cohesion of the socialist camp. The government of the Grand Coalition had also emphasised that its policy of reconciliation with the East could only be brought to fruition in collaboration with Moscow, and that the FRG therefore had no wish to promote hostility or exploit differences between the Eastern states. However, the credibility of these assurances suffered from statements issued during the period by high government officials, including members of the Cabinet, which were patently incompatible with the spirit of the declared policy.[13] In addition, and more importantly, the actual development of relations between Bonn and the Eastern states during 1967–68 was liable to cause concern in Moscow. While the Soviet-German dialogue ran into the doldrums, diplomatic relations were established with Romania and resumed with Yugoslavia, the two least conformist of the socialist states in Europe (if one disregards Albania). Thus, whatever the declared goals or intended results of Bonn's *Ostpolitik*, the FRG's increased activities in Eastern Europe during those years had contributed to the further disintegration of the Soviet empire. It is this development, with its climax during the Czechoslovakian crisis of 1968, that explains the consistent efforts of the Brandt government to reach an accommodation with Moscow before anything else.

However, this did not imply a neglect of relations with other states in the

East, since another basic feature of West German negotiating behaviour in the period after 1969 was the way it recognised and utilised the interdependence of the three levels of *Ostpolitik*. Thus, the policy makers in Bonn considered it essential to overcome the impasse in inter-German relations not only because this reflected the major preoccupation in their policy towards the East, but also because they viewed such a step as necessary if they were to reach a better understanding with the other Eastern states, especially the Soviet Union. However, the mechanism of interdependence was seen by the Brandt government as working both ways: while it believed that no real breakthrough in Bonn's policy of reconciliation with the East could be achieved without *some* progress in its relations with the GDR, the fundamental policy concept outlined above was based on the assumption that significant headway on the two other negotiating levels, especially the one with Moscow, could not fail to influence the position of the East German leadership.[14] The correctness of this basic assumption would seem to be borne out by the striking correlation during 1969–71 between on the one hand steps toward improved Soviet-West German relations and on the other hand East German initiatives implying, at least ostensibly, a more forthcoming attitude towards Bonn.

In December 1969 Bonn reached agreements with both Moscow and Warsaw to initiate confidential bilateral talks aiming at a normalisation of their mutual relations. The first meeting between West German and Soviet diplomats was held on 8 December, while talks between the FRG and Poland were scheduled to start in early February 1970. In this situation Walter Ulbricht, seeing that Moscow and Warsaw were preparing themselves for a serious exchange of views with West Germany, decided to propose that negotiations between Bonn and East Berlin begin as early as January 1970. In a draft treaty submitted to Bonn in connection with this initiative, the East German side insisted on *diplomatic* relations and the exchange of ambassadors between the FRG and the GDR.[15]

This move confronted the West German government with the problem how to achieve a direct, confidential negotiating contact with the SED leadership without accepting the demands for recognition under international law contained in the latest East German proposal. In his report on the State of the Nation, presented to the *Bundestag* on 14 January 1970, Chancellor Brandt refrained from commenting on the East German draft treaty, but emphasised that formal agreements between the two German states could be the result but not the starting point of negotiations. Brandt hinted at the flexibility of the West German position when he acknowledged the importance of the political equality of Bonn and East Berlin and expressed understanding for the East German preoccupation with 'certain abstract formalities' – obviously a reference to the recognition issue. But he also indicated that the concessions

Bonn might be willing to grant in that direction were dependent on whether the East German leaders were prepared to consider making substantive improvements in the conditions of those who suffered most severely from the division of Germany. Brandt made it perfectly clear that there would be no progress if the East German side demanded that negotiations be limited to its latest draft treaty.[16]

The next move from the East German side followed on 19 January 1970, when, in a press conference, Mr. Ulbricht confirmed his willingness to negotiate without explicitly insisting on his own draft treaty as a basis for talks with Bonn. At the same time Ulbricht's pronouncements suggested that the East German leadership wished to wait for the first results of the Soviet-West German negotiations before committing itself any further.[17] The West German government immediately denounced the East German attitude as an effort to delay the development of East-West negotiations and emphasised that it did not expect any progress in its relations with the GDR from a continued *public* exchange.[18] A few days later Mr. Brandt sent a letter to his East German counterpart, Mr. Willi Stoph, proposing that the two governments open negotiations on the renunciation of force in their mutual relations.[19]

This exchange indicates that the new leadership in Bonn was anxious to ensure a minimum of parallel procedures in its *Ostpolitik*, at least in the sense that it wished to transform public dialogues with all three main partners in the East into confidential *pourparlers*. At the same time the basic concept underlying Brandt's Eastern venture presumed a major breakthrough in relations with Moscow as a *sine qua non* for progress on the two other negotiating levels. Consequently, at the end of January 1970 Chancellor Brandt's closest associate, State Secretary Egon Bahr, was sent to Moscow with far-reaching instructions. In the course of three intensive rounds of talks and negotiations between the two delegations, headed by Messrs. Bahr and Gromyko respectively, a breakthrough on the most important level of Bonn's *Ostpolitik* was eventually achieved.[20] But long before this the East German leadership – under the influence, one assumes, of the increased contact between Moscow and Bonn signified by Bahr's arrival in the Soviet capital – was prompted to take a new initiative. On 12 February 1970 the GDR suggested a top level meeting between the heads of the two German governments for the purpose of safeguarding peaceful coexistence and normal relations between the two German states.[21] Two such meetings were held in the course of that spring; the first, on 19 March, in the East German town of Erfurt; the second, on 21 May, in the West German town of Kassel. These spectacular encounters failed to bridge the gap between the fundamental positions of the two sides: on the one hand the West German insistence on *substantive* normalisation, through improvements in the daily life of people in divided Germany; on the other hand East German demands for *formal* normalisation, through international recognition of the GDR, as the necessary first step toward better relations between the two German states.[22] While Brandt and Stoph agreed to continue the exchange of views, no concrete arrangements were made for a new meeting. Indeed, the East Germans asserted that Bonn apparently needed 'time to reflect upon its attitude and arrive at a realistic standpoint'.[23]

All the same, the two meetings gave to both sides *something* in terms of their specific priorities. Erfurt and Kassel offered the East German leaders opportunities for demonstrating the 'statehood' of the GDR and its equality with West Germany. These events could thus be presented as steps toward the *formal* normalisation of relations between the two German states.[24] The West German leadership had been able to establish personal contact with the head of the East German government. It had formulated in some detail what it meant by *substantive* normalisation and presented a twenty-point programme to that effect at Kassel. Mr. Brandt could – and did – claim that these were the necessary first steps on the long road to a better understanding with the leaders of the GDR. Finally, the agreement to pursue the dialogue opened up the prospect that in due course more regular confidential negotiations could be conducted on that most difficult level of West German *Ostpolitik*.[25]

The two meetings also satisfied some of the immediate policy requirements of the two sides. East Berlin could now claim that it was keeping in line with the general trend towards *détente* in East-West relations, whereas Bonn had demonstrated its good will towards East Germany, thereby enhancing the overall credibility of its Eastern policy. This was essential if the intensified negotiations with Moscow were to succeed.

In these negotiations the fundamental dilemma facing the West German side was the need to acknowledge and respect in unambiguous terms the prevailing territorial situation in Central Europe without, however, formally anticipating a German peace treaty or prejudging the rights and responsibilities of the Victor Powers regarding Germany as a whole. This was important since the Four Power rights were a legal framework suggesting the continued relevance of the concept of a united Germany, which Bonn was anxious to retain as a symbol of its hope of achieving self-determination and some form of unity for the whole German people[26]

The West German negotiators in Moscow – led most of the time by Mr. Egon Bahr and in the final stage by Foreign Minister Walter Scheel – succeeded in safeguarding West Germany's basic interests relating to these long-term perspectives of German unity and self-determination. Three features of the treaty signed in Moscow by Chancellor Brandt and Premier Kosygin on 12 August 1970 were of special importance in this context:

1) The treaty text nowhere used the term *recognition* about the prevailing territorial and political status quo in Europe, since the Soviet side had dropped its original demand for *de jure* recognition of the GDR.[27]

2) While the treaty expressed the unqualified respect of the contracting parties for the territorial integrity of all states in Europe within their present frontiers, the latter were declared 'inviolable', not unalterable, which left open the prospect for their future alteration (or even elimination) by the free consent of all concerned.

3) In connection with the signature of the Moscow treaty, Foreign Minister Walter Scheel addressed a separate 'letter on German Unity' to his Soviet colleague, Mr. Gromyko, which the latter accepted. By doing so, the Soviet government acknowledged the fact that the treaty did not conflict with the stated objective of the FRG 'to work for a state of peace in Europe in which the German nation will recover its unity in free self-determination'.[28]

As for the relations between the two German states in the immediate future, the agreement with Moscow implied a confirmation of the West German concept that some measure of *détente*, and thus an improvement of relations between the GDR and the FRG, were a necessary precondition for the formal admittance of the GDR to the international arena.[29]

The stipulations of the Moscow treaty clearly fell short of original East German hopes. Since the GDR leadership needed some time to adapt itself to the new situation, it was only natural that the pause on the inter-German level of Bonn's *Ostpolitik* should continue after the Soviet-West German agreement. However, in late October 1970, when a treaty between Bonn and Warsaw appeared to be within reach, and the Four Power negotiations on Berlin had entered a more intensive stage, the East German leaders again decided to show at least a greater flexibility *vis-à-vis* Bonn. They agreed to begin confidential talks with representatives of the FRG without insisting on the fulfilment of any prior conditions by Bonn. A first meeting between State Secretaries Egon Bahr and Michael Kohl took place on 27 November 1970.[30]

By the end of 1970 the Brandt/Scheel government could draw up an impressive balance sheet: on two of the three levels of *Ostpolitik* protracted negotiations had led to formal agreements, a treaty on the normalisation of relations between the FRG and Poland having been signed in Warsaw on 7 December 1970.[31] While the Moscow and Warsaw treaties had sparked off a rather heated domestic controversy in West Germany, they were hailed by governments and peoples in East and West – with the conspicuous exception of the People's Republic of China – as milestones on the road to peace and security in Europe. On the third, most complicated level of inter-German relations, Bonn had succeeded in transforming a public dialogue, marked by mutual recriminations, into a confidential exchange of views without prejudging the outcome of future negotiations in the process.

In 1971, Bonn's most immediate preoccupations in the realm of *Ostpolitik* were focused on Berlin, since one of the calculated consequences of Mr. Brandt's Eastern venture was the strengthening of East Germany's international position. In the light of previous experience it could be expected that, unless adequate international guarantees had been instituted before, the SED leadership would exploit any up-grading of its international status in order to exercise its 'sovereign rights' in a way liable to undermine the viability of the Western enclave in Berlin. West Germany therefore had a paramount interest in contractual arrangements safeguarding uninhibited access to the city, and the preservation of those numerous ties that in the course of postwar years had developed between the FRG and West Berlin.[32] This consideration was one of the reasons why the West German government had insisted on the connection between ratification of the Eastern treaties and a satisfactory agreement on Berlin.

From the very outset it was recognised by all concerned that, while a contractual agreement regulating conditions in and around Berlin could only be negotiated among the Four Victor Powers, its proper implementation required the co-operation of both German states. The confidential talks between representatives of the two German governments, initiated at the end of 1970, could undoubtedly smooth the way for the practical arrangements that would have to be agreed upon between Bonn and East Berlin to ensure the satisfactory functioning of a Four Power accord. However, for a considerable time progress along that line had been prevented by East German attempts to use the confidential contacts with Bonn to pre-empt the result of the Four Power negotiations.[33] Bonn, for its part, indicated a willingness to talk about traffic problems in general, with a view to concluding a comprehensive treaty or a set of agreements which should supplement each other. But the West German side refused to commit itself on issues pertaining to the Berlin traffic that would anticipate any arrangements on principles by the Four Powers.[34]

The contacts between State Secretaries Bahr and Kohl continued more or less regularly, and in March 1971 they were supplemented by similar talks between East German authorities and representatives of the *Senat* in West Berlin. But apart from the limited re-opening of telephone communications between East and West Berlin they yielded no substantive results in the course of the spring and summer. However, it was only with the quadripartite agreement on Berlin, signed by the representatives of France, the Soviet Union, the United Kingdom and the United States on 3 September 1971, that a solid foundation was laid for negotiations between the two German states. In the immediate aftermath of the Four Power agreement, though, the relations between Bonn and East Berlin were marred by new difficulties, which in turn can be mainly attributed to the fact that the Berlin accord implied significant Soviet concessions at the expense of the GDR. The following three points were of special importance in this context:

1) The quadripartite agreement established the ultimate responsibility of the

Four Powers for the civilian traffic on the access routes to West Berlin, and prescribed that such traffic would be 'unimpeded', 'facilitated so as to take place in the most simple and expeditious manner' and would 'receive preferential treatment'.[35] This amounted to a reversal of the Soviet position on the issue of East German 'sovereignty', upheld until early May 1971, and all but eliminated the possibility that the GDR leaders would exploit their physical control over the access routes to West Berlin for political purposes of their own choosing.

2) The Four Power agreement reasserted that West Berlin was not 'a constituent part' of the FRG and was not governed by it. But at the same time it decreed that the ties between West Berlin and the FRG would be maintained and developed. This provision conflicted with persistent East German attempts to neutralise and, if possible, liquidate *all* West German influence in the former German capital.

3) The Soviet government agreed to improve the communications between West Berlin and its immediate surroundings, specifically committing itself in the agreement to enabling permanent residents of West Berlin to visit East Berlin, as well as other areas of the GDR, 'under conditions comparable to those applying to other persons entering these areas'.[36] This regulation touched on a very sensitive spot of the East German leadership: its fear of 'contagion' and 'infiltration' from the West, the West Berliners being the category of 'Westerners' entertaining the most persistent and legitimate wishes to enter the GDR, and this in relatively great numbers and at as frequent intervals as possible.

The quadripartite agreement presupposed the implementation of detailed arrangements between the FRG and the GDR, as well as between the *Senat* of West Berlin and the appropriate East German authorities, before it came into force.[37] Since the wording of certain provisions in the agreement was ambiguous the GDR leadership, now headed by Erich Honecker who had succeeded Ulbricht as First Secretary of the SED in early May, tried to neutralise or modify some objectionable elements in the Four Power accord by interpretations of its own. A total impasse in the inter-German talks was broken only at the end of September 1971, when the East German side desisted from its efforts to use the ambiguous term 'the competent German authorities' in the quadripartite agreement [38] as a way of dealing separately with Bonn and West Berlin on the issue of transit regulations.[39]

On the whole, the scope for East German obstruction on *substance* was distinctly circumscribed by the rather detailed provisions of the Four Power accord, and in general it would seem true to say that the delaying tactics of the GDR were eventually overcome thanks to the concurring Soviet and West German interest in the speedy conclusion of an overall deal between East and West in Europe. This interest was clearly manifested during a meeting between Soviet Party leader Brezhnev and Chancellor Brandt at Oreanda in the Crimea, from 16–18 September 1971.[40] Thus, in the course of the ensuing inter-German negotiations the West German side managed to secure the essentials of the concessions that had been wrung from Moscow by the three Western powers. On 13 December 1971, immediately after the initialling of the inter-German agreements on Berlin [41], the West German government initiated the process of ratifying the Moscow and Warsaw treaties.[42]

5 The diplomacy of inter-German normalisation

First and foremost, the result of the Berlin negotiations implied increased safety for West Berlin, and alleviated West German concern for the future of the Western enclave at a time when Bonn envisaged a strengthening of the international position of the GDR. In addition, the Berlin agreements, especially the facilities provided for improved contact and communication between West Berlin and the GDR, opened up prospects for a substantive normalisation at the very place where the abnormal situation created by the division of Germany had been most evident. Thus, the Berlin agreements could be viewed as a vindication of the basic concept underlying the *Deutschlandpolitik* of the Brandt/Scheel government: the Soviet interest in the formalisation of the status quo in Europe had been successfully utilised to elicit Moscow's consent to some improvement in the relations between the two German states, even though the results were modest measured by the yardstick of popular aspirations.

The Bonn government, however, was under considerable domestic pressure to obtain a more far-reaching accommodation between the FRG and the GDR than that implied by a 'satisfactory' Berlin agreement. If it is true, as claimed by one well informed observer of the West German scene, that the Brandt/Scheel government originally contemplated establishing a link between ratification of the Eastern treaties and a comprehensive inter-German accord, these plans were abandoned prior to the signature of the Moscow treaty.[43] But over and above a *bilateral* deal with Bonn, stabilising prevailing conditions in Central Europe, Moscow had shown some interest in a *multilateral* formalisation of the status quo in Europe through the proposed conference on security and co-operation in Europe (CSCE). Bonn also had some leverage *vis-à-vis* Moscow in this context, as suggested by the stipulation in the preliminary Soviet-West German draft agreement of May 1970 (the 'Bahr paper'), which committed both sides to promoting the CSCE.[44] Not only was West German participation in the conference essential; the FRG had also demonstrated its ability to influence the attitude of other Western states on that issue.[45] And since the Anglo-Saxon powers at least continued to display a marked lack of enthusiasm for the proposed conference, West German help was obviously needed if it were to materialise within the foreseeable future. For some time therefore the Bonn government entertained the idea of another *quid pro quo*: West German consent to the initiation of multilateral preparations for the CSCE would be made dependent on some measure of inter-German accommodation. This particular bargain, however, turned out to be impractical, mainly as a result of French policy. Having eventually been converted to the notion that multilateral negotiations within a pan-European framework were a good thing, Paris was critical of the kind of inter-German connection that the Bonn government was interested in. In early 1971 the French government let it be known that, for its part, it was satisfied with a Berlin agreement as the only precondition of such multilateral consultations, thereby establishing a kind of lowest common denominator in the West on the CSCE issue, and a position which was subsequently adopted by NATO at the ministerial meeting in Lisbon, from 3–4 June 1971.[46]

By the autumn of 1971, the only purpose relevant to inter-German normalisation for which Bonn could exploit the Soviet interest in the *multilateral* formalisation of the status quo, was the speeding up of East Germany's implementation of the quadripartite agreement on Berlin. This was clearly one of the tasks before Chancellor Brandt when, in mid-September 1971, he went to the Crimea to meet the Soviet Party leader. The communiqué from the Oreanda meeting and its timing suggest that the interdependence of the preparations for the CSCE and the pace of inter-German negotiations was recognised by both sides. The meeting occurred at a time when the implementation of the Berlin agreement seemed to be jeopardised by a deadlock in the inter-German negotiations, due to East German intransigence. In view of these circumstances, the fact that the Oreanda communiqué reaffirmed the conditions for a general normalisation of FRG-GDR relations in the same terms as previously agreed between Moscow and Bonn could be interpreted as a signal to East Berlin to be more forthcoming.[47] On the other hand, the passage on the CSCE in the Oreanda communiqué indicates that the West German side increased its support for the CSCE proposal by committing itself to consultations with Moscow, the Western allies and other European states in order to *hasten* the convening of such a conference.[48]

These observations, however, should not obscure the fact that in the autumn of 1971 Soviet interest continued to be focused on the *bilateral* arrangement with Bonn, and that the main incentive for Moscow to intervene in the inter-German negotiations seemed to be the wish to see the Moscow treaty ratified.[49] Indeed, the limitations of West Germany's leverage *vis-à-vis* Moscow on the issue of the CSCE was demonstrated during Foreign Minister Scheel's visit to the Soviet capital in late 1971. On that occasion

Mr. Scheel tried in vain to persuade the Soviet government to sign the final protocol of the Berlin agreement as soon as the impending inter-German accord had been reached. His argument that, in view of the joint NATO position, the multilateral preparation of the CSCE would otherwise be delayed, could not dispose the Soviet government to commit itself formally to the agreed concessions in Berlin so long as its bilateral deal with Bonn had not been validated on the part of the FRG.[50]

At the turn of the year, with the Berlin negotiations concluded and the ratification process in Bonn initiated, a new stage in West Germany's *Deutschlandpolitik* was approaching, a stage in which the SPD/FDP government, having spent most of its diplomatic leverage *vis-à-vis* the Soviet Union, would be facing the question of how far it was possible to promote further measures of inter-German normalisation by way of Moscow. During spring 1972, however, this problem did not make itself felt immediately, due to unexpected developments in the FRG that, after the conclusion of the main East-West negotiations but prior to the formal validation of their result, tended to enhance West Germany's bargaining position.

By March 1972 the erosion of the parliamentary support of the Brandt/ Scheel government had reached a point where the ratification of Bonn's Eastern treaties appeared to be seriously endangered, thereby refocusing the attention of governing elites on the substance of the original East-West package deal of 1970–71. In that situation the Soviet leadership, having a major stake in the completion of that deal and being well aware of the intricacies of the political situation in the FRG, displayed an inclination to make Chancellor Brandt's task easier.

The leader of the CDU/CSU, Mr Rainer Barzel, had claimed that the treaties failed to tackle what he termed the central problem: the situation of the Germans in Germany. Consequently, in his list of demands that had to be satisfied in order to enable the opposition to vote for the treaties, the issue of increased communication and freedom of movement between the FRG and the GDR loomed large.[51]

The Soviet leaders exerted themselves to invalidate the main objections of the CDU/CSU through different initiatives of their own.[52] But the assured prospect of inter-German normalisation required the collaboration of Mr. Honecker and his associates in the GDR leadership. Since the East German side adapted its policy to the requirements of Moscow[53], tangible elements of substantive inter-German normalisation were at the very last moment included in the East-West package deal. In the preamble of the treaty on traffic questions between the FRG and the GDR initialled by State Secretaries Bahr and Kohl on 12 May 1972, both parties committed themselves to striving for 'normal, good-neighbourly relations'.[54] The treaty itself, to become effective only after ratification of the Moscow and Warsaw treaties, provided for significantly improved facilities of communication between the two German states. In connection with the initialling of this agreement, the East German government issued a declaration announcing that, once the treaty had come into force, a number of measures would be introduced facilitating the entry of FRG citizens into the GDR and – the most significant novelty – enabling East German citizens to visit West Germany for urgent family reasons.

Developments during the spring of 1972 seemed to vindicate a basic principle of Chancellor Brandt's diplomacy *vis-à-vis* East Berlin that had been clarified in his first State of the Nation message[55], namely that steps towards the *formal normalisation* of FRG-GDR relations must be accompanied by measures implying *substantive normalisation* in terms of improved conditions in the life of those most immediately affected by the division of Germany. The general traffic agreement between the FRG and the GDR combined both processes: it was the first state treaty to be concluded between the two German states and in that sense undoubtedly signified a measure of formal normalisation; at the same time it provided for distinct practical improvements in the relations between people on both sides of the dividing line. In addition, the more forthcoming attitude of the SED, which had facilitated the speedy conclusion of the traffic agreement, also seemed to open up prospects for further progress along that same line. During a visit to Bulgaria in mid-April 1972 the East German Party leader, Mr. Honecker, declared himself ready, once the Moscow and Warsaw treaties had been ratified, to enter into negotiations with Bonn aiming at an overall normalisation of mutual relations. This offer was accepted by Chancellor Brandt.[56]

However, the fact that inter-German normalisation had been explicitly tied up with the East-West package deal of 1970–71 made the prospect for further progress somewhat uncertain. As Mr. Brandt's Eastern venture was approaching a new stage in 1972, the basic question emerged of how far the reorientation of East German policy had been the result of deference to Soviet wishes, and how far it was due to the strengthening of contacts between the two German states. It was generally recognised that in the course of over forty encounters between the two negotiating teams, headed by Messrs. Bahr and Kohl respectively, a foundation of mutual confidence had been established which augured well for the future of inter-German relations. Nor could there be any doubt that developments since 1970 had encouraged popular hopes on both sides, conferring upon the process of inter-German normalisation a momentum of its own, which neither of the two German governments could disregard. Yet, how significant were these forces compared with those opposing a *rapprochement*? This crucial question could be fully clarified only in a new phase of East-West relations, during which the specific incentives for inter-German understanding, emanating from the mutual desire of the Soviet and West German governments to validate the package deal of 1970–71, would no longer be operative. That new phase began when, on 17 May 1972, the West German *Bundestag* ratified the Moscow and Warsaw treaties.

Notes

[1] Cf. above p. 8. See also Peter Bender, *Die Ostpolitik Willy Brandts*, pp. 41f and 74f.

[2] The Social Democratic Mayor of West Berlin, Mr Klaus Schütz, expressed this idea succintly when in 1969 he asserted, 'Der Gegenstand der Ostpolitik ist Deutschland selbst' ('The subject matter of *Ostpolitik* is Germany itself'). See Klaus Schütz, 'Ostpolitik mit oder gegen Moskau?', in Kurt Birrenbach *et alia, Aussenpolitik nach der Wahl des 6. Bundestages* (Aktuelle Aussenpolitik), C. W. Leske Verlag, Opladen 1969, p. 122.

[3] For excerpts from Egon Bahr's speech of 15 July 1963, see H. Siegler *Wiedervereinigung und Sicherheit Deutschlands* vol. 1, 5th ed., Bonn-Zürich-Wien 1964, p. 311f.

[4] The following paraphrase is based on the author's conversation with Egon Bahr on 12 December 1971. For similar views expressed in 1969 by another leading West German Social Democrat, see Klaus Schütz, *op. cit.*, p. 123.

[5] While this fact is beyond dispute, Wolfgang Wagner's assertion that 'an evaluation of Soviet policy and of the Eastern European situation did not play a significant role in the decision [to launch a new Eastern policy] seems exaggerated. Cf. Wolfgang Wagner, 'Towards a new political order: German *Ostpolitik* and the East-West realignment' *Internatonal Journal* vol. xxvii, no. 1 (Winter 1971–72), p. 19f. Undoubtedly, there was a strong yearning for action among the rank and file of the SPD and the FDP, nursed through long years of immobilism on the part of the CDU/CSU, particularly *vis-à-vis* East Germany. Yet, the actual decision to inaugurate a new policy must be seen in the light of the more conciliatory attitude of Moscow and its allies toward the West, as evinced in numerous declarations since the Warsaw Pact meeting in Budapest in March 1969. See also Peter Bender *op. cit.*, p. 75.

[6] For a discussion of the problems facing Bonn in terms of domestic adaptation to the realities in Europe, see below p. 35f.

[7] This is borne out by a comparison between official declarations from the period of the Grand Coalition, for example that of 13 October 1967 in *Texte zur Deutschlandpolitik* (hereafter cited *Texte)* vol. ii, pp. 9ff., and the first government declaration of Mr Brandt as Federal Chancellor on 28 October 1969, *Bulletin* no. 132/1969. For the text as delivered, see *Protokoll der 5. Sitzung des Deutschen Bundestages vom 28. Okt., 1969.* Reprinted in: *Texte* vol. iv, pp. 9ff.

[8] Cf. President Nixon's inaugural address, 20 January 1969, and his speech at the NATO council meeting commemorating the 20th anniversary of the Atlantic alliance on 10 April 1969, *Department of State Bulletin*, vol. ix, no. 1546, pp. 121ff and no. 1547, pp. 351ff.

[9] For a perceptive analysis by a high-ranking West German official reflecting this concern see Paul Franke, 'Sicherheitsprobleme im Lichte des Moskauer Vertrags' *Europa-Archiv* 24/1970, p. 867 ff.

[10] See government declaration of 28 October 1969 referred to in note 7.

[11] See below, Chapter 3, p. 62.

[12] Cf. Thomas Oppermann, 'Deutsche Einheit und europäische Friedensordnung: Perspektiven nach dem Moskauer Vertrag' *Europa-Archiv* 3/1971. English translation in *Survival*, July 1971.

[13] For the official policy of the Grand Coalition see, for example, Kiesinger's declaration before the Bundestag on 14 June 1967, *Texte* I, vol. i pp. 71f. On the diverging views of other leading West German officials see my *Peace in Europe*, p. 106.

[14] See above, p. 32. On the interdependence of the three levels of West German Ostpolitik see P. Bender, *Die Ostpolitik Willy Brandts*, p. 102.

[15] For the text of the East German draft treaty see *Neues Deutschland*, 21 December 1969. English translation in *Survival*, May 1970, pp. 173f.

[16] See Brandt's speech of 14 January 1970, *Texte*, vol. iv, p. 201 ff. The text of this speech was enclosed with a letter to the Chairman of the Council of Ministers of the GDR, Mr Willi Stoph, on 22 January 1970. This constituted the West German reply to Mr Ulbricht's initiative of 17 December 1969, cf. note 15.

[17] See Walter Ulbricht's exposé before the international press on 19 January 1970, *Aussenpolitische Korrespondenz* 1970, No. 4.

[18] See declaration of the Federal government on 19 January 1970, *Texte*, vol. iv, pp. 275f.

[19] Chancellor Brandt's letter to Chairman Stoph, 22 January 1970, *Erfurt March 19, 1970. A Documentation.* (Press & Information Office of the Government of the FRG, Bonn 1970) p. 5.

[20] Cf. Chapter 1, p. 8.

[21] *Aussenpolitische Korrespondenz* No. 8, 23 February 1970.

[22] For a full documentation of the two German top meetings in 1970 see *Erfurt March 19, 1970. A Documentation* and *Kassel May 21, 1970. A Documentation*, also published by the Press & Information Office of the Government of the FRG.

Toward the end of the Kassel meeting Mr Brandt again hinted at the willingness of his government to trade steps towards substantive normalisation for measures leading to the international recognition of the GDR, when he said: '...You continually say that the Government of the German Democratic Republic allows itself to be guided by the interests of the people ... but we lack concrete information about what this is supposed to signify in relation to the contractual arrangements between our two countries. And yet it must be possible, Mr Chairman, to give us an answer to our questions. *Were we to receive such answers I am convinced that in the course of time the problem you characterise as international recognition of the German Democratic Republic can also be settled ...*' (my italics), *Kassel May 21, 1970. A Documentation*, p. 52. Mr Stoph's response, however, suggested no inclination on his part to enter such a bargain.

[23] See Communiqué on the Meeting of the Council of Ministers of the GDR on 25 May 1970, *ibid*, p. 78.

[24] Cf. Chairman Stoph's Report of 21 March 1970 to the 16th Assembly of the *Volkskammer* in East Berlin, in *Erfurt March 19, 1970*, pp. 81ff.

[25] See the statement by the Federal Chancellor before the Federal Press Conference on 22 May 1970 in Bonn, in *Kassel May 21, 1970* pp. 25f. For the twenty point programme presented by the West German side at Kassel see *ibid.*, pp. 84ff.

[26] Cf. *The Treaty of August 12, 1970*, pp. 85–6.

[27] See the text of the Moscow treaty, *ibid.*, pp. 7–9. The fact that the Soviet Union dropped the demand for 'the recognition of the GDR in international law' can be deduced from point 6 in the draft agreement which resulted from the Bahr-Gromyko negotiations (the so-called 'Bahr paper'), *ibid.*, p. 17. See also the official West German 'Reflections' on the treaty, *ibid.*, p. 86.

[28] *Ibid.*, p. 10.

[29] This seems to be borne out by guideline 7 in the 'Bahr paper', *ibid.*, pp. 17–18. While this point of the 'Bahr paper' was not incorporated in the Moscow treaty itself, it remained operative as one of the 'statements of intent' which were to guide the policies of the two governments; see *ibid.*, p. 63.

[30] A joint statement issued simultaneously by the two German governments on 29 October 1970 announced that agreement had been reached to initiate an official exchange of views on questions 'the settlement of which would serve the cause of détente in Central Europe and which were of interest to both states' (*Neues Deutschland*, 30 October 1970). For the communiqué after the first meeting between Bahr and Kohl see *Texte* vol. vi, p. 220.

[31] The text of the treaty between the FRG and Poland, as well as other relevant documents are published in *The Treaty between the Federal Republic of Germany and the People's Republic of Poland*. Press and Information Office of the Federal Government [Wiesbaden 1971].

[32] Cf. Arnulf Baring, 'Das Ziel: Gute Nachbarschaft mit Ost und West' *Die Zeit*, 29 October 1971.

[33] See below, Chapter 3, pp. 58ff.

[34] Cf. Report on the State of the Nation presented by Federal Chancellor

Willy Brandt to the German *Bundestag* on 28 January 1971, *State of the Nation 1971*, p. 8.

[35] *The Quadripartite Agreement on Berlin*, p. 12.

[36] *Ibid.*, p. 13.

[37] See *ibid.*

[38] *Ibid.*, pp. 12 and 16.

[39] Cf. W. Wagner, 'Aussichten der Ostpolitik nach dem Abschluss der Berlin-Verhandlungen' *Europa-Archiv* 3/1972, p. 82 and note 5.

[40] See the communiqué issued after the Oreanda meeting, *Bulletin* No. 136, 21 September 1971. For evidence suggesting Soviet representations in East Berlin with a view to hastening the pace of inter-German negotiations see Chapter 1, p. 61.

[41] For the texts of these agreements which were initialled on 11 December and signed on 17 and 20 December 1971 respectively, see *Bulletin*, no. 183, 11 December 1971.

[42] See *Bulletin* no. 186, 15 December 1971.

[43] W. Wagner, *op. cit.*, *Europa-Archiv* 3/1972, p. 84.

[44] See *The Treaty of August 12, 1970*, p. 18.

[45] The communiqué after the NATO ministerial meeting in Brussels in December 1969 envisaged for the first time the convening of the CSCE after progress had been achieved in the impending bilateral negotiations. This shift in the collective Western attitude was mainly due to the fact that Chancellor Brandt had taken on the role of chief promotor of the conference idea within NATO. See *Department of State Bulletin* vol. lxi, no. 1592, pp. 628 ff.

[46] *Ibid.*, vol. lxiv, no. 1670, pp. 819 ff.

[47] *Soviet News* no. 5606, 21 September 1971.

[48] See *ibid.* In the relevant portion (guideline 10) of the 'Bahr paper', which had been incorporated in the final Soviet-West German agreement as a declaration of intent, the corresponding commitment was formulated in less specific terms: 'to do everything that depends on them [the contracting parties] for its [the CSCE's] preparation and successful prosecution'. Cf. *The Treaty of August 12, 1970*, p. 18.

[49] See above, Chapter 1, p. 17 and below Chapter 3, p. 61

[50] See interview with Walter Scheel shortly before his trip to Moscow, published in *Die Zeit*, 19 November 1971, under the heading 'Der Mann neben Brandt'. Cf. also R[olf] Z[undel], 'Moskau bleibt hart, Nach Scheels Visite: die Sowjets fordern Parallelität' *Die Zeit*, 3 December 1971.

[51] See Barzel's speech in the Bundestag on 23 February 1972, *Bulletin* No. 26, 25 February 1972, p. 322. For the other demands of the CDU/CSU and Soviet reactions see above, Chapter 1, p. 18.

[52] See above, Chapter 1. pp. 18f.

[53] For the details of this change of course on the part of the GDR, see below, Chapter 3, pp. 62f.

[54] *Treaty between the German Democratic Republic and the Federal Republic of Germany on Questions Relating to Traffic*, unofficial (East German) translation, p. 5.

[55] See above, p. 37.

[56] For the text of Erich Honecker's speech in Sofia on 18 April 1972, see *Aussenpolitische Korrespondenz* No. 17/1972, 26 April 1972, p. 126. Chancellor Brandt's acceptance of the East German offer to pursue negotiations was expressed publicly in his speech before the *Bundestag* on 10 May 1972, see *Bulletin* No. 68, May 11, 1972, p. 961.

3 East Germany and the European Détente

1 Major determinants of policy

The constraints determining the *Deutschlandpolitik* of the GDR were similar to those of the ruling Bonn coalition in the sense that both German governments wanted to widen their freedom of manoeuvre, but at the same time saw the need of safeguarding their power at home and obtaining the support of their principal allies. More significant, however, than these similarities were the differences in conditions for policy formulation and implementation prevailing in Bonn and East Berlin respectively. Two striking differences are worth emphasising.

The first and most obvious one was the disparity in the negotiating positions of the two German states, due to the relative diplomatic isolation of the East German state as compared with the Federal Republic. It has been demonstrated how Bonn utilised the interdependence of the three levels of its Eastern policy, specifically the impact of Soviet-West German negotiations on East German official attitudes. The GDR leadership, however, disposed of no similar leverage: far from being able to conduct substantive negotiations with West Germany's allies, it lacked any direct lines of communication with the major Western powers.

The other difference was related to the nature of the two main constraints determining the scope for independent action on the part of the two German states: deference to the wishes of the main allies and concern about the domestic power situation. With regard to both these factors the East German leadership was confronted with problems that were qualitatively different from those Bonn had to cope with in connection with its *Ostpolitik*. Like all governing elites in the states belonging to the Soviet alliance the GDR leadership lacked explicit popular legitimation of its rule and therefore had to rely ultimately on Moscow's support. This crucial dependence not only distinctly circumscribed its freedom of manoeuvre in foreign policy, but also determined its very survival as a ruling elite.

This is not to imply that the East German leaders could ever disregard the wishes and moods of the population in the GDR. The opposite is true, if only because popular attitudes were of decisive importance for the kind and degree of backing that the SED leadership needed and could expect from Moscow. But given the lack of overall popular support, it was this relationship, rather than the feelings and preferences of the masses *per se*, that for a

53

long time seemed to be a major preoccupation of the SED leadership. With regard to the attitude of the East German population one can distinguish four main levels stretching in a more or less continuous spectrum from (1) suppressed resistance via (2) resigned submission and (3) unenthusiastic collaboration to (4) explicit consent and support of specific measures. The closer the ruling elite believes the situation to be to the latter end of the spectrum the greater its effective freedom of action *vis-à-vis* Moscow. At the same time the GDR leadership was able to exploit its lack of popular support in order to impose certain restrictions on Moscow's freedom of action.

While this connection between the level of domestic popularity and Soviet support is characteristic of the position of most ruling elites in Eastern Europe, the GDR leadership was faced with specific problems on account of two circumstances.

Firstly, the SED had to concern itself not only with consolidating its power in East Germany, but also with the very nature of the social and political order under its rule. To ensure that this be unchallenged was essential if some measure of popular backing for the regime were to be engendered and sustained. In addition, it constituted a *sine qua non* for Moscow's support, since the East German leaders could be certain of Soviet protection only if they succeeded in consolidating the position of the GDR as a viable socialist state.[1]

Secondly, the rulers in East Germany could use neither of the two means by which other East European elites tried to win consent and support from the broad masses of the population: the appeal to nationalist feelings and the experimentation with liberalisation or even some form of democratisation of the political and social system. Thus, the SED was left with measures conducive to the improvement of living conditions as virtually the only way of stabilising its domestic position.[2]

In the course of the 1960s the consolidation of the GDR as a viable political and social entity had progressed significantly. The erection of the Berlin Wall in August 1961 has generally been recognised as a turning point in this connection. The physical barrier which thereafter prevented the massive exodus of East Germans to the West was an essential condition for the impressive performance of the East German economy during the last decade. But 'the second German *Wirtschaftswunder*' would not have been possible without the introduction of major economic reforms in 1963–64.[3]

These developments had important psychological repercussions in both East and West. Western acquiescence in the division of Germany and Berlin, as well as the rising standard of living in the GDR, made the East German population increasingly inclined to reconcile itself with its lot and to make the best of a difficult situation. In the Federal Republic the Wall and the improvement of material conditions in East Germany helped to initiate a process of rethinking, which implied a gradual public recognition of the realities in Central Europe. This process in turn eventually produced a corresponding reorientation of West German policy. Yet, it was the shift in Bonn's official stand and the concomitant activation of its *Ostpolitik* that confronted the East German leadership with the unpleasant prospect of being forced to choose between two equally distasteful alternatives: either opposing the trend toward *détente* in Europe, thus risking isolation within its own camp, or else adapting itself to the general trend and thereby exposing the GDR to influences that, it was feared, would tend to erode the power basis of the ruling elite.[4] This remained the basic dilemma of the SED during the late 1960s and early 1970s.

2 The course of official policy since 1969

The period between the formation of the government of the Grand Coalition in Bonn in December 1966 and the Czechoslovak crisis in the summer of 1968 was characterised by a general trend towards East-West *détente* in Europe, a development that was watched with a great deal of concern by the East German leaders.[5] Yet, during those years the East German leadership managed to avoid the most dangerous contingencies for two main reasons. Firstly, the ambiguity of the Kiesinger government's Eastern policy, especially regarding its relations with the German Democratic Republic, enabled Walter Ulbricht to discard the West German initiatives as ultimately serving the same revanchist goals as those pursued by previous West German governments. The only difference, he argued, was that the new leaders tried to use more subtle and therefore more dangerous means.[6] Secondly, Mr. Ulbricht could count on the support of the Soviet leadership in this matter, since Moscow was worried about the destabilising effect of Bonn's new *Ostpolitik* upon conditions in Eastern Europe at large and displayed an increasingly rigid and apprehensive attitude towards the West.

By the end of 1969, however, the situation had changed in both these respects. The GDR leadership was now confronted with far more consistent West German efforts at reconciliation with the East and these in turn encountered a positive response in virtually all East European capitals, including Moscow.

Furthermore, the Soviet leadership, having managed to consolidate conditions in Czechoslovakia largely in accordance with its wishes, seemed to favour more rather than less co-operation between East and West in Europe, although only within distinct limits and under Moscow's close supervision. Thus, the terrifying alternative prospects of *isolation* or *infiltration* posed themselves to the East German leaders more plainly than ever before.

In this situation the GDR leadership embarked on a flexible strategy. It implied paying lip-service to the commonly agreed Eastern positions and included some more or less spectacular East German initiatives, like the proposal of December 1969 for a state treaty between the GDR and the FRG as a first step towards normalisation. The main purpose of these moves seems to have been to gain time to bring East Germany's policy in line, ostensibly at least, with the general trend toward a reduction of tensions and better East-West understanding. At the same time, however, the leaders in East Berlin showed themselves as uncompromising as ever towards Bonn in terms of its substantive demands. Indeed, their opposition was even stepped up, since the normalisation of relations between the two German states proposed by Mr. Ulbricht in December 1969 foresaw not only Bonn's recognition of the GDR under international law, but also revision of the Federal Republic's ties with the Western allies.[7]

This East German strategy, which also included the initiative for a top meeting between the leaders of the two German governments, led to the encounters of Messrs Brandt and Stoph in Erfurt and Kassel in the spring of 1970. While these meetings were of more than symbolic significance, they did not effect any change in the East German leadership's unwillingness to accept the *quid pro quo* suggested by Mr. Brandt, implying the trading of progress towards the international recognition of the GDR for measures substantively normalising and improving relations between the two German states. At the time, East Berlin argued that the latter would be tantamount to 'peaceful counter-revolution' unless preceded by full diplomatic recognition of East Germany on the part of the Federal Republic.

The Moscow treaty of 12 August 1970, between the Soviet and West German governments, caused considerable concern and embarassment in East Berlin. Official pronouncements in August and September 1970 indicated, how difficult it was for Mr. Ulbricht and his associates to adapt themselves to the new situation and how they attempted to influence developments after the signature of the treaty in accordance with their own preferences.

The main bones of contention from the East German point of view seem to have been the following:

1) The demand for West Germany's diplomatic recognition of the GDR had not been fulfilled in the Moscow treaty: on the contrary, by accepting the guidelines contained in the 'Bahr paper' as an agreed common basis for future policy, the Soviet government had tacitly acknowledged the West German view that, due to the continuing validity of Four Power rights for all Germany, it was *legally* impossible for the Federal government to recognise formally any German boundaries and thus the GDR.[8] Furthermore, Moscow had also displayed an inclination to accept or at least acquiesce in the West German contention that inter-German normalisation was a higher priority than the international recognition of the GDR.[9]

2) The reaffirmation, during bilateral negotations with Bonn, of Four Power responsibilities on the part of Moscow implied a threat against East German interests, especially in Berlin. This threat became even more serious in view of the West German insistence on a political link between ratification of the Moscow treaty and a satisfactory agreement on Berlin.[10]

3) Finally, there is ample evidence that the prospect of a new dynamic stage in East-West relations opened up by the Moscow treaty did not please the East German leaders at all. They were obviously worried lest a marked increase in contact, exchange and communication between Eastern and Western Europe occur without any prior stabilisation of their power position through international recognition of the GDR.

The divergence of Soviet and East German interests was clearly demonstrated when the SED leadership tried to deduce from the signature of the Moscow treaty that both Bonn and third countries were now obliged to establish full diplomatic relations with the GDR.[11] Moscow showed its disapproval of the East German stand by deleting the pertinent sentences in the Russian translation of the East German declaration.[12] If, in an initial phase, the SED leadership had tried to make its consent to Moscow's new line of policy dependent on the fulfilment of its own demands, the attempt had apparently failed.[13] At a meeting of the Political Consultative Committee of the WTO on 20 August 1970 the GDR delegation seems to have been induced to subscribe to the common formula describing the Moscow treaty as a major step toward *détente* and normalisation in Europe.[14]

This, however, did not mean that the GDR leadership had reconciled itself to following Moscow's lead and giving up its specific demands: on the contrary, the evidence indicates that the East German leaders, having ostensibly accepted the Moscow Treaty, redoubled their efforts to prevent a further Soviet-West German *rapprochement* and anything that remotely suggested an opening up of Eastern Europe to Western influence.[15] Thus, they displayed an adamant position *vis-à-vis* West Germany and decried proposals for economic and technological co-operation between the two German states as attempts at capitalist infiltration of the GDR. The assertion that this represented a danger as serious as the open attacks of the imperialists against the GDR was probably meant not only as a reminder to the East German population to beware of contacts with the treacherous West Germans; it could also be interpreted as a warning to Moscow that its policy was liable to endanger the stability of the GDR and thus the whole Soviet empire in Eastern Europe.[16] While the situation of the East German leaderhip was precarious, it managed to avoid complete isolation from the mainstream of Soviet policy during the two months following the signing of the Moscow treaty. A common basis for the official attitudes of Moscow and East Berlin during this period was the campaign against the political link between ratification of the treaty and an agreement on Berlin.[17]

By the end of October 1970, however, the East German leaders had once more changed their strategy toward Bonn. While they had hitherto argued that the dialogue begun at the top meetings in Erfurt and Kassel could only be pursued if the West German side changed its basic position, the SED leadership now agreed to initiate confidential talks without insisting on the fulfilment of any prior conditions. This new development must be seen against the background of the headway that the West German negotiators were making in Warsaw[18] and the greater Soviet inclination to reach an understanding with the West on Berlin.[19]

The East German initiative was probably a gesture of deference to Moscow but it was also an attempt to inject a GDR presence into the process of East-West negotiations so as to influence it more directly.[20] With the intensification of the Four Power talks on Berlin the leaders of the GDR must have been anxious to use every opportunity to safeguard their primary interests not only *vis-à-vis* West Germany, but also in relation to Moscow, since Soviet preoccupations had shown themselves not be to fully in accord with those of Mr. Ulbricht and his associates. The opening up of direct negotiations between the two German states gave the SED leadership some additional leverage, which it utilised in an attempt to pre-empt the outcome of the Berlin talks.

In the face of Western unity and determination to insist on certain essentials in a Berlin agreement, the Soviet leadership had, by late autumn 1970, begun to feel its way towards a compromise in the Four Power negotiations.[21] This change of tactics caused friction with the East German leaders, since Moscow was anxious to induce them to modify their adamant stand. The Soviet-East German differences were demonstrated, when, on 8 November 1970, Mr. Ulbricht spoke of the possibility of a transit agreement with the FRG, provided the activities of other states in West Berlin that were in conflict with the legal status of that city were ended.[22] The international status of West Berlin was at that time the subject of heated controversies in the Four Power negotiations; but Soviet Foreign Minister Mr. Gromyko had shortly before indicated to the American government that the Soviet side did not demand the complete elimination of the West German presence in West Berlin as a precondition of an agreement. Mr. Ulbricht's statement was therefore interpreted as a rebuttal directed primarily against Moscow.[23]

When, at the end of November 1970, East Berlin finally decided to implement its previously announced intention to initiate confidential talks with Bonn, there was no sign of a mellowing of the GDR's *substantive* position. The claim to an unqualified East German right to control civilian traffic on the access routes to West Berlin was demonstratively emphasised through the prolonged harassment of traffic to West Berlin on the occasion of a meeting of the CDU/CSU parliamentary group in West Berlin. In this action the GDR received full backing on the part of the Soviet Union.

A top-level meeting of the Warsaw Pact leaders was convened in East Berlin on 2 December 1970 to iron out differences between the GDR and its allies. The meeting agreed on some formulas that clearly reflected Soviet rather than East German priorities. Thus, the joint communiqué expressed the hope that a mutually acceptable agreement would be reached in the Four Power talks on Berlin. Among the criteria for such an agreement were mentioned 'the needs of the population of West Berlin' along with 'the legitimate interests and sovereign rights of the GDR'.[24] Yet, subsequent interpretations of this formula by Mr. Ulbricht and Soviet representatives made it clear that the East German leaders had managed to uphold their claim of an exclusive right to control the civilian traffic between the Federal Republic and West Berlin.[25] Since this position was quite unacceptable to the Western powers, there remained a substantial gap between East and West on this issue alone.

During the following weeks the acute difficulties of the GDR leadership in its relations with the other Warsaw Pact countries were temporarily alleviated as a result of the unrest along the Polish Baltic coast. These events seem to have caused significant concern in Moscow regarding the ability of the Polish and East German ruling elites to prevent uncontrollable chain reactions.

A moratorium on the Soviet Union's active Western policy followed in early 1971, a period during which the correctness of the foreign policy pursued since 1969 was apparently re-examined within the Soviet power elite. The East German leadership seems to have been actively engaged in this process of challenge and response within the leadership of the CPSU, trying to reverse or at least to modify the general line of Moscow's policy in accordance with its own preference for a continuation of confrontation with the West.[26]

Walter Ulbricht used this period of uncertainty in Soviet policy to consolidate the SED's position *vis-à vis* Moscow in several different ways. In the field of ideology he reasserted his claim to originality by emphasising, at the 15th SED Central Committee Plenum, that the East German party was developing its own indigenous model of socialist construction (*das entwickelte gesellschaftliche System des Sozialismus*). His thesis that the process of creating a developed system of socialism in the GDR included certain elements of transition to *communism* constituted a direct challenge to Moscow's ideological supremacy.[27]

With regard to the all important issue of *Deutschlandpolitik* the East German stand was marked by an intensification of GDR proposals.[28] On 4 February 1971 Mr Stoph hinted at the possibility of agreements between the

59

Senat of West Berlin and the GDR that would serve to better the living conditions in the city; this suggested that the East German leadership wished to open an additional level of negotiations dealing with Berlin.[29] The aim of this move was clearly to secure a further margin of manoeuvre in the process of East-West negotiations, which, in spite of the events in Poland, was expected soon to regain its momentum.

By the middle of February 1971 the basic line of Moscow's Western policy had been reconfirmed, and the Soviet leaders showed some inclination to accept, at least tacitly, the link between ratification of the Moscow and Warsaw treaties on the one hand and an agreement on Berlin on the other.[30] Shortly afterwards the first signs of East Germany's adaptation to that situation appeared. On 24 February 1971 the head of the East German government, Mr. Stoph, sent a letter to the Mayor of West Berlin, Mr. Klaus Schütz, the contents of which were made public and indicated that the GDR leadership was no longer attempting to use negotiations with the *Senat* of West Berlin for the purpose of undermining the responsibilities of the Four Powers or of pre-empting the outcome of their negotiations.[31]

Subsequent developments make it plausible to assume that the final endorsement of Brezhnev's and Kosygin's Western policy at the 24th Congress of the CPSU brought to a head an internal leadership crisis in the GDR, which resulted in Walter Ulbricht being ousted from the leading position in East Germany. His departure from the post of First Secretary of the SED was officially announced on 3 May 1971. The changes in policy introduced by the new leadership under his successor, Erich Honecker, indicated that ideological issues had been one of the main bones of contention between Ulbricht and Moscow. The 16th Central Committee Plenum of the SED demonstratively acknowledged the ideological leadership of the CPSU and dropped the ambitious model concept of 'the developed societal system of socialism' introduced by Ulbricht.[32]

At the same time there is some evidence that the Berlin question also played an important role in the events leading to the reshuffle at the top of the East German power elite.[33] The SED under Mr. Honecker adopted a stand, with regard to both the Berlin negotiations and the international recognition of the GDR, that was distinctly more in accordance with Soviet priorities than the previous East German position.[34] This is not to imply that the East German official attitude towards West Germany became less adamant. The opposite was the case, a logical consequence of the shift in the SED leadership, since Mr. Honecker had been the main proponent of a policy of strict demarcation (*Abgrenzung*) *vis-à-vis* Bonn.[35] It is sometimes overlooked, however, that this uncompromising stand made the East German leaders more, rather than less, susceptible to Soviet pressure. The developments of 1970–71 show that the more the East German leaders insisted on a strict policy of *Abgrenzung* toward West Germany, the harder was it for them to exploit their domestic weakness and exposed position in attempts to forestall an understanding between the Soviet Union and the Federal Republic. Similarly, the more unchangingly hostile East Berlin's official relations with Bonn, the more limited was its scope for independent manoeuvres and initiatives in the process of East-West negotiations.

Walter Ulbricht's reaction to the emerging Soviet-West German *rapprochement* had been a blend of tactical flexibility and substantive rigidity *vis-à-vis* both Bonn and Moscow. His successor was unable to pursue that policy not only for the reason that he lacked Ulbricht's personal authority, but also –and perhaps more significantly–because external conditions–the maturing of an overall East-West deal in Europe–forced him to adapt the East German stand to the requirements of *détente* and co-operation.

Against this background, it is not surprising that the Soviet Union succeeded in eliciting the concessions from the SED leadership that were necessary for a mutually acceptable agreement on Berlin with the three Western powers.

The quadripartite agreement on Berlin, signed on 3 September 1971, implied an improvement of East Germany's international status in as much as the existence of the GDR was for the first time officially acknowledged by the Western powers. On the other hand, the Four Power accord significantly limited the GDR's freedom of action in the most sensitive and crucial area of its foreign policy.

Erich Honecker, it is true, argued with Moscow that 'for the first time the sovereignty of the GDR's relations with the other German state and West Berlin has been confirmed in the quadripartite agreement by the three Western powers.'[36] But in his reply to Honecker's message Leonid Brezhnev did not commit himself to this East German interpretation of the agreement, which clearly went beyond the tacit consensus achieved between the Four Powers on the status of the GDR.[37] Keeping in mind the latent divergence of interest reflected in this exchange, it is possible to view subsequent actions and declarations of the GDR in terms of the following immediate policy objectives: firstly, to demonstrate and assert East Germany's role as an independent or at least semi-autonomous actor in the process of East-West negotiations; secondly, to limit the impact of the seemingly unavoidable opening toward the West inherent in the Berlin agreement; and thirdly, to exploit the momentum created by that accord for a further improvement in the international standing of the GDR.

If the intransigence displayed at times by the GDR in the inter-German negotiations during autumn 1971 was designed to further the first of these goals, the outcome can hardly have been gratifying to the SED. The Soviet leadership, it appears, intervened in East Berlin in order to accelerate the pace of these negotiations, and the performance of the East German leaders tended, under the circumstances, to jeopardise rather than promote the image of the GDR as a self-assertive actor in the international arena.[38] If anything the developments between September and December 1971 confirmed the impression that Moscow's influence on East Germany's foreign policy had increased, and that the GDR had been forced to trade an improvement in international status against a further limitation of its scope for independent action.

As for the two other goals mentioned above, the GDR had reason to be more satisfied with what was achieved in the course of 1971. East Germany's behaviour in the negotiations with the FRG and West Berlin for the implementation of the quadripartite agreement suggests that the SED was anxious to keep visits of 'westerners' to the GDR, within distinct bounds. The settlement of that issue in the inter-German agreements of December 1971 represented a compromise, which took into account the sensitivity of the GDR leaders as far as increased communication between East and West was concerned.[39] Finally, with regard to the international standing of the GDR, the SED appears to have been operating on the assumption that time was on its side. After the quadripartite agreement the GDR leadership displayed marked confidence in an impending breakthrough toward international recognition of East Germany[40], and with the completion of the Berlin negotiations at the end of the year its spokesmen doubled their efforts to denounce the 'Scheel doctrine' as doomed to failure and patently incompatible with the generally recognised principles of equality and non-discrimination.[41]

Until early 1972 the East German leadership under Erich Honecker had sought to combine the necessary minimum of substantive concessions in favour of East-West *détente*, dictated by the requirements of Soviet policy, with a stance of relentless enmity towards 'the imperialistic FRG'. These seemingly contradictory attitudes were reconciled by the differentiation between peaceful coexistence of states with differing social systems on the one hand, and 'the objective process' of demarcation between socialism and capitalism on the other. There could be no doubt, however, that the SED leadership was anxious to stress the militant aspect of its stance: while *détente* had finally been acknowledged, *Abgrenzung* was writ large.[42]

A significant shift in East German policies and attitudes occurred in the course of spring 1972. On 23 February 1972 the GDR leadership announced the temporary implementation, during Easter and Whitsun, of the travel arrangements for West Berliners provided for in the Berlin agreements, even though the latter had not yet come into force.[43] This decision, presented by East Berlin as a 'good-will gesture' fostering European *détente*, was followed be further steps suggesting a greater East German readiness to allow a number of substantive improvements in the contact and communication of the people of the two German states. The shift was also reflected in the tone of

62

authoritative East German pronouncements, which even began to emulate some of the central concepts of an inter-German *modus vivendi* used by Bonn.

The highlights of this development were two speeches delivered by Erich Honecker on 10 March and 18 April 1972 respectively, as well as the speedy and satisfactory conclusion of the negotiations between State Secretaries Kohl and Bahr about inter-German traffic questions. In his speech of 10 March 1972, given at the international spring fair in Leipzig, Honecker referred to the polarisation of political forces in the FRG in connection with the *Bundestag* debate on the ratification of the Moscow and Warsaw treaties. He emphasised that only the ratification of these treaties would make it possible for the inter-German agreements to come into force and 'to open up a development leading to a peaceful living together, side by side (*friedlichem Nebeneinander*), between the GDR and the FRG, that is to say ... in the end to good-neighbourly relations ...'.[44].

If the marked emphasis on the prospect of a peaceful *Nebeneinander* represented a distinct novelty in the pronouncements of the SED, Mr. Honecker became even more conciliatory when, on 18 April 1972, during a visit to Sofia, he spoke on the same subject. This time his perspective included the possibility of togetherness (*Miteinander*) 'in the interest of the citizens of both states'.[45] The prospects for inter-German normalisation mapped out by the East German Party leader became more definite when in early May the GDR consented to considerable improvements in contact and communication between people in the two German states, once the East-West package deal had been validated.[46]

The change of attitude was thus perceptible. Yet, the question remained as to how far the new East German stance represented more than a tactical adaptation to the immediate requirements of the international situation of spring 1972, emanating from the unfinished East-West package deal.

While any attempt by an outside observer at providing conclusive evidence on this crucial issue is at present doomed to failure, it should be possible to set out the general frame of reference within which the question of East Germany's future relations with the West was being tackled by the leaders of the GDR.

3 'Abgrenzung' and peaceful coexistence: East-West co-operation from the viewpoint of the SED.

An assessment of official East German viewpoints regarding relations with the West presupposes some familiarity with the publicly proclaimed overall outlook of the ruling elite in the GDR, its views about the major tasks confronting the SED in the fields of domestic and international politics and about their interrelation.

Ever since the 7th Party Congress in April 1967 two aspects of East Germany's efforts to build a socialist society had been emphasised: firstly, the increasing international significance of the East German 'model', and secondly, its interdependence with the endeavours of other socialist countries, especially those of the Soviet Union.[47] Whereas the first element seemed to dominate the thinking of Walter Ulbricht, the latter was given increasing prominence and emphasis in the course of 1971, notably after Honecker's accession to the leading post in the party hierarchy. Thus, official pronouncements in connection with the 8th Party Congress in mid-June 1971 emphasised the importance of the CPSU's guidance and the further strengthening of fraternal ties with the Soviet Union and other socialist states.[48] The reorientation of economic policy in the direction of stricter central control, initiated in early 1971 and endorsed by the 8th Party Congress in June of that year, also implied that the SED had adapted itself more closely to the prevailing trends in the Soviet Union.[49]

These shifts, however, did not lead to a reformulation of the central task confronting the SED. This remained the development and completion of a socialist society in the face of the scientific and technological revolution, which is considered a decisive factor influencing all social action in the current historical period, Indeed, to establish the proper connection between socialist construction and the scientific-technological revolution was declared to be the major concern of the party. It is hardly a coincidence that a recent East German study devoted to the interdependence of foreign and domestic policy stressed that all problems related to the scientific-technological revolution could only be solved in close collaboration with other members of the socialist community, not in isolation and even less by striving for 'the alleged assistance' of imperialist countries.[50]

This position was clearly in line with the prevailing theory of *Abgrenzung*, but it raised the question of the scope for 'mutually advantageous co-operation' between countries with different social and political systems, to use the formula derived by the socialist states from their theory of peaceful coexistence. Mr. Honecker, it is true, had attempted to present the two concepts as compatible by arguing that *Abgrenzung* was a precondition for relations of peaceful coexistence.[51] This assertion, however, only begged the basic question about the nature of East-West relations in a period which, according to the clearly expressed preferences of Moscow, should be marked both by the distinct demarcation and consolidation of the socialist camp and the growth in East-West co-operation.

Peaceful coexistence is a concept of fundamental importance for understanding the ideological basis of the policies of the socialist states in the present historical era. At the same time its meaning has proved to be sufficiently loose for it to suit different political circumstances. Peter C. Ludz has observed that the term 'has been applied to denote (1) a form of class struggle, (2) the ongoing non-military contest with imperialism, and (3) a positive effort at co-operation'. He concludes very properly that 'these definitions can be used in a great variety of combinations and weights to fit any specific situation, turning the notion of "peaceful coexistence" into a magical umbrella.'[52] As a consequence, an analysis of the term's application can at times provide clues to the policy preferences of the ruling elites in different socialist states or of those entertained by the leadership in the same country at different times.

Virtually all Communist parties, including the SED, tend to present *the objective reality of peaceful coexistence* as an achievement of the socialist commonwealth in its prolonged and continuing class struggle with capitalism (or imperialism), a fact reflecting a global balance of forces that is said to be increasingly favourable to the socialist states.[53] In accordance with this overall view, a recent East German study argued that the capitalist countries have been induced by the victories of socialism to wage the unavoidable global contest between the two systems under conditions of 'peaceful coexistence' rather than 'active war' or 'cold war'.[54] Not only economic competition but also economic collaboration are included under the concept of the class struggle, and peaceful coexistence, as the present form of that struggle, does not, therefore, exclude co-operation between states with different social systems.[55] Similarly, the East German leadership put forward the view that *Abgrenzung* between the socialist system of the GDR and the capitalist system of the FRG did not preclude co-operation between the two German states.[56]

The ideological distinctions of the SED have always been complicated by the continuing relevance and frequent use of the concept of the German 'nation'. These difficulties were exacerbated when the Brandt/Scheel government began to employ this term in a consistent effort to counteract the trend towards alienation between East and West Germany.[57] In early 1970, therefore, Mr. Ulbricht, whose public utterances until then had been marked by a persistent adherence to the concept of *one* German nation, was finally induced to differentiate between 'the socialist German nation state', the GDR, and 'the capitalist NATO-state' with 'limited national sovereignty', the FRG.[58] His successor, Erich Honecker, went even further by distinguishing between the 'socialist' nation of the GDR and the 'bourgeois' nation of the FRG.[59] Thus, *Abgrenzung* henceforth acquired an additional national dimension, in the sense that the SED leadership exerted itself to portray the GDR as the only *genuine* bearer of German nationality.

As long as peaceful coexistence was used mainly to denote *the objective reality* of the present state in the relations between capitalism and socialism, the term presented no major problems to the SED, since it could be reconcil-

65

ed both with an increasingly strict understanding of *Abgrenzung* and a pugnacious definition of co-operation. Lately, however, another aspect of peaceful coexistence has been given greater prominence on the part of East Germany's allies, namely its importance as *a deliberate and systematic policy*, dependent on the political will of both sides.[60] Leonid Brezhnev's speech before the 24th Congress contained some phrases that appeared to reflect the interest of at least some important forces within the party leadership in the long term consolidation of relations with the capitalist countries, particularly the United States.[61] When the leaders of the Warsaw Pact states at their meeting in Prague on 25–26 January 1972 formulated a number of 'basic principles of European security and relations among states in Europe', the one on 'peaceful coexistence' concluded with the following assertion: 'Renouncing war as a means of pursuing their policy, the European states belonging to different social systems can and *must* build their relations on the basis of *agreement and co-operation* in the interests of peace'.[62] This appeal, while ostensibly addressed to all European states, can be interpreted as an implicit exhortation to the forces within the socialist states opposing closer East-West co-operation. It can hardly be a coincidence that after the Prague meeting the SED leaders were at pains to present their own performance on the European scene, which unquestionably was marked by greater conciliatoriness, as an 'active policy of peaceful coexistence' in implementation of the commonly agreed programme.[63]

It is important to keep in mind that the adaptation of the SED's general frame of reference was accompanied by changes in domestic practices clearly designed to satisfy East German aspirations for greater freedom of movement, better social services and a further improvement of the material standards of the individual citizen.[64] Seen in conjunction, these developments as well as the stepped-up efforts to gain international recognition[65], suggest that in 1972 the leadership of the SED was preparing the ground for an era of gradually evolving East-West collaboration, which presupposed a consolidation of its rule through recognition abroad and popular satisfaction at home. Conceivably, the East German leaders hoped that a period of closely supervised, but successively enlarged contact with the West, could, if successfully managed, open up an escape from the dilemma that had confronted them ever since the inception of the European *détente*. Coupled with an improvement in its legal status and self-confidence at home *a controlled opening to the West* might eventually help them to contain once and for all the double risks of isolation and infiltration.

Notes

1 Peter Bender *6 × Sicherheit: Befürchtungen in Osteuropa* Köln & Berlin 1970, p. 67.

2 *Ibid.* pp. 74–75. See also Peter Christian Ludz, 'The German Democratic Republic from the Sixties to the Seventies. A Socio-Political Analysis' *Occasional Papers in International Affairs* no. 26 (Harvard University, Center for International Affairs, November 1970) p. 29f. See also Thomas A. Baylis 'In Quest of Legitimacy' *Problems of Communism* March–April 1972, pp. 48ff. He argues convincingly that 'manipulative participation' from above can be used as a means to elicit popular support. It would seem, however, that this instrument has a supplementary function only and presupposes a minimum of 'performance-based' legitimacy.

3 Cf. Melvin Croan, 'After Ulbricht: the End of an Era?' *Survey* vol. 17 (1971) no. 2, p. 83.

4 For a thoughtful discussion of 'the East German regime's two deepest anxieties' see Melvin Croan, 'Czechoslovakia, Ulbricht and the German Problem' *Problems of Communism* vol. xviii, no. 1, (Jan.–Feb. 1969) pp. 1ff. Peter Bender also refers to this basic East German dilemma in his *Die Ostpolitik Willy Brandts oder die Kunst des Selbstverständlichen*, p. 39.

5 See my *Peace in Europe*, pp. 58f, 66f.

6 Cf. *ibid.*

7 This is borne out by a number of East German pronouncements. See, for example, *Neues Deutschland*, 27 and 30 December 1969.

8 See Georg Ferdinand Duckwitz, 'Die Wende im Osten' *Aussenpolitik* 1970/11, p. 649f.

9 See *Der Vertrag vom August 12, 1970*, pp. 16f. Cf. also Egon Bahr's comment *ibid.* p. 64f.

10 At the same time the link afforded East Berlin some leverage with regard to the process of implementing the deal between Moscow and Bonn, which it did not fail to utilise during ensuing months. See above, Chapter 2, p. 44.

11 See 'Erklärung des Ministerrates der DDR zum Abschluss des Vertrages. zwischen der UdSSR und der BRD' in *Neues Deutschland*, 15 August 1970.

12 Cf. *Pravda*, 15 August 1970.

13 Cf. Gerd Hagen, 'Die DDR und der Moskauer Vertrag' *Aussenpolitik* 1970/11, p. 663.

14 See communiqué issued after the meeting of the Political Consultative Committee of the Warsaw Treaty Member States in Moscow on 20 August 1970, *Soviet News* no. 5557, 25 August 1970.

15 See Willi Stoph's address on the occasion of the 21st anniversary of the foundation of the GDR on 6 October 1970, *Neues Deutschland*, 7 October 1970.

16 See editorial entitled 'Unsere Zukunftsgewissheit – ihr Dilemma. Über

einige Motive der imperialistischen Propaganda gegen die Wirtschaftspolitik der DDR' *Neues Deutschland*, 9 September 1970. Cf. Hagen, *op. cit.* p. 664

[17] Cf. above, Chapter 1, p. 14. For an emphatic East German indictment of the link see, for example, speech by Mr. Stoph on 6 October 1970, *Neues Deutschland*, 7 October 1970.

[18] See above, Chapter 2, pp. 40.

[19] Cf. above, Chapter 1, pp. 14.

[20] That the East German decision was due at least partly to Soviet represent-ations is suggested by the fact that the new position had been announced on the day of Mr. Gromyko's visit to East Berlin, 29 October 1970.

[21] Cf. above, Chapter 1.

[22] See excerpts of Mr. Ulbricht's television conversation in *Europa-Archiv* 1/1971, p. D 16.

[23] Cf. Gerhard Wettig, 'Die Ost-Berlin Konferenz der Warschauer-Pakt Staaten und die Aussichten für eine befriedigende Berlin-Regelung' *Berichte des Bundesinstituts für Osteuropäische und Internationale Studien*, 6/1971, p. 1.

[24] *Pravda*, 4 December 1970. For English text see *Soviet News* no. 5572, 8 December 1970. Mr. Brezhnev, in a speech at Erevan on 29 November 1970, had even spoken of 'the wishes' of the West Berliners as a guideline for an agreement.

[25] See Walter Ulbricht's address before the Central Committee of the SED, 9 December 1970, *Neues Deutschland*, 10 December 1970. For reports to the effect that Moscow supported Ulbricht's claim see Joachim Schwelien, 'Eine zweite Eiszeit ist nicht in Sicht' *Die Zeit*, 22 January 1971.

[26] See the evidence referred to in Richard Löwenthal's analysis 'Kreml am Kreuzweg. Stalin's Schatten liegt über der Ostpolitik' *Die Zeit*, 19 February 1971.

[27] The text of Ulbricht's address before the 15th SED Central Committee Plenum on 28 January 1971 is printed in *Neues Deutschland*, 30 January 1971. For an interpretation of its implications see Ilse Spittmann, 'Warum Ulbricht stürzte' *Deutschland-Archiv* 6/1971.

[28] See Walter Ulbricht's New Year address on 31 December 1970, where he repeated the suggestion of a transit agreement between the GDR and the FRG. Cf. also his speech before the 15th SED Central Committee Plenum on 28 January 1971, in which he referred not only to imperialist forces, but also to more realistic tendencies in the FRG. *Neues Deutschland*, 1 and 29 January 1971.

[29] *Aussenpolitische Korrespondenz* no. 7, 15 February 1971.

[30] See above, Chapter 1, pp. 15.

[31] The text of Willi Stoph's letter to Klaus Schütz, 24 February 1971, was published in *Neues Deutschland*, 26 February 1971. In this document the East German government proposed negotiations with the *Senat* of West

Berlin in order to enable citizens of West Berlin to visit the GDR, including its capital. Then followed the sentence that could be interpreted as an East German acceptance of the Four Power prerogatives in Berlin: 'Eine Vereinbarung in dieser Frage kann verständlicherweise in dem Falle verwirklicht, werden, wenn Vereinbarungen über andere West-Berlin betreffende Fragen, die in entsprechenden Verhandlunger beraten werden, in Kraft gesetzt sind'. For a thoughtful interpretation of East Germany's *Deutschlandpolitik* prior to the 8th Congress of the SED see Marlies Jansen, 'Deutschlandpolitik und VIII. Parteitag' *Deutschland-Archiv* 8/1971.

32 See 'Vom hohen Rang der 16. Tagung' *Neues Deutschland*, 6 May 1971. The 16th SED Central Committee Plenum completely revised the agenda for the impending 8th Congress of the SED, making it appear less pretentious in terms of ideological aspirations. Cf. Oldenburg, *op. cit.*, pp. 3–4; also Harald Ludwig, 'Die SED vor dem VIII. Parteitag' *Deutschland-Archiv* 6/1971, pp. 585ff.

33 Mr. Abrasimov, at that time Soviet ambassador to East Germany and Soviet representative at the Four Power negotiations sent a telegram of congratulations only to Mr. Honecker and not to Mr. Ulbricht on the occasion of the latter's departure from the post of First Secretary of the SED. This has generally been interpreted as an indication of major differences between Moscow and Ulbricht over Berlin. The fact that it was on the crucial issue of responsibility for unimpeded civilian traffic on the access routes to West Berlin that the Soviet Union made the decisive concession to the Western side, and that it did so immediately after the announcement of the change in the top leadership of the SED also points in this direction.

34 See announcement issued after the visit of an East German party and government delegation to Moscow on 18 May 1971, *Aussenpolitische Korrespondenz* no. 21, 24 May 1971.

35 In his first major speech as First Secretary of the SED Erich Honecker argued forcefully for complete *Abgrenzung* as a *precondition* for relations of peaceful coexistence between the two German states. See his address before the 16th SED Central Committee Plenum on 3 May 1971, *Neues Deutschland*, 4 May 1971.

36 See message from Erich Honecker to Leonid Brezhnev, 8 September 1971, published in *Second Session of the Central Committee of the Socialist Unity Party of Germany, Berlin, 16 and 17 September 1971* (Information Service of the Socialist Unity Party of Germany) 1/1971, p. 72.

37 In his reply to Honecker, dated 10 September 1971, Brezhnev confined himself to the statement that the agreement took 'fully into account the sovereign rights and interests of the German Democratic Republic' and contributed to 'an increase of the international authority of the socialist German state, its role and influence in international affairs'. *Ibid.*, p. 74.

[38] See communiqué of 1 November 1971, issued after Leonid Brezhnev's unofficial visit to East Berlin, 30–31 October 1971. This emphasised the importance of a speedy conclusion of current inter-German negotiations and of the initiation of multilateral preparations for an all-European conference. *Pravda*, 2 Nov. 1971. Cf. also Erich Honecker's declaration on 5 November 1971 announcing the GDR's interest in concluding negotiations on Berlin before the end of November. This new sense of urgency on East Germany's part clearly contrasted with its attitude prior to Brezhnev's visit.

[39] For the texts of the inter-German agreements initialled on 11 December 1971 see *Bulletin* no. 183, 11 December 1971.

[40] See text of East German memorandum of 15 October 1971, submitted to the UN General Assembly, and resolution adopted by the foreign policy committee of the East German Parliament on 15 October 1971, *Aussenpolitische Korrespondenz* no. 43, 26 October 1971. Cf. also Manfred Feist, 'Die Autorität der DDR wächst trotz imperialistischer Manöver' *Einheit* 9/1971.

[41] See Erich Honecker's declaration at the 4th Central Committee Plenum of the SED on 17 December 1971, *Neues Deutschland*, 18 December 1971. Cf. also statement of a spokesman of the GDR Ministry of Foreign Affairs, published in *Foreign Affairs Bulletin* (GDR) no. 1, 6 January 1972, p. 6.

[42] See Honecker's speech referred to in note 41; also his address before representatives of the *Nationale Volksarmee* on 6 January 1972, *Neues Deutschland*, 7 January 1972.

[43] *Aussenpolitische Korrespondenz* no. 9, 1 March 1972, pp. 62f.

[44] For excerpts from the original German version of Honecker's speech see *Aussenpolitische Korrespondenz* no. 11, 15 March 1972. The quotation in the text is taken from the official East German translation, printed in *Foreign Affairs Bulletin* (GDR) no. 9, 23 March 1972, p. 62.

[45] *Aussenpolitische Korrespondenz* no. 17, 26 April 1972, p. 126. The importance attributed to this formula is borne out by the fact that Honecker repeated it *verbatim* in an interview with *Neues Deutschland* on 25 April 1972, presenting it at the same time as consistent with the decisions of the SED's 8th Congress and the co-ordinated foreign policy of the socialist states. See *Foreign Affairs Bulletin* (GDR) no. 13, 2 May 1972, p. 95.

[46] See above, Chapter 2, pp. 45f.

[47] See Walter Ulbricht, 'Die gesellschaftliche Entwicklung in der DDR bis zur Vollendung des Sozialismus' *VII. Parteitag der SED*, Berlin 1967.

[48] See Report of the Central Committee of the SED to the 8th Congress delivered by Erich Honecker, *Neues Deutschland*, 16 and 17 June 1971. For a West German appraisal cf. Hans Dietrich Sander, 'Reduktion statt Sachlichkeit' *Deutschland-Archiv* 7/1971, p. 683.

[49] Cf. Kurt Erdmann 'Abkehr vom bisherigen Modell des Ökonomischen Systems des Sozialismus' *Deutschland-Archiv* 8/1971, pp. 816f.

[50] Werner Hänisch & Joachim Krüger, 'Zur Dialektik von Innen- und Aussenpolitik in der Strategie und Taktik des SED' *Deutsche Aussenpolitik* 3/1971 p. 446.

[51] Cf. above, note 35.

[52] Peter C. Ludz, 'Continuity and Change since Ulbricht' *Problems of Communism*, March–April 1972, p. 61.

[53] Cf. 'Report of the Central Committee of the CPSU to the 24th Congress ..., delivered by Leonid Brezhnev ... March 30, 1971', in *24th Congress of the CPSU* (Novosti Press Agency Publishing House, Moscow 1971) pp. 9, 36. For a recent East German statement to that effect, see for example, the speech by Hermann Axen, member of the Politbureau and secretary of the Central Committee of the SED at the 5th plenary session of the Central Committee of the SED, 27–28 April 1972; *Aussenpolitische Korrespondenz* no. 18, 4 May 1972.

[54] Cf. K. H. Domdey, 'The efforts of the GDR to establish normal economic relations with capitalist states: A case of peaceful coexistence' *Co-existence* vol. 9 (1972) no. 1, p. 60.

[55] *Ibid.*, p. 61.

[56] See report of the Central Committee of the SED to the 8th Party Congress delivered by Erich Honecker, in *VIII. Parteitag der SED, Berlin, 15–19 Juni 1971*, pp. 19 ff. Cf. also his address before the 4th plenary session of the Central Committee of the SED, 17 December 1971, *Neues Deutschland*, 18 December 1971.

[57] Cf. above, Chapter 2, p. 34.

[58] See Walter Ulbricht's introductory speech at the international press conference convened in East Berlin on 19 January 1970, *Neues Deutschland*, 20 June 1970.

[59] See Honecker's report to the 8th Congress of the SED referred to in note 56. Cf. also Peter C. Ludz, 'Zum Begriff der "Nation" in der Sischt der SED, Wandlungen und politische Bedeutung' *Deutschland-Archiv* 1/1972, pp. 17 ff.

[60] Evgeny Chossudovsky distinguishes 'the existence of a world system of socialist states ... as an irreversible fact of political life' from 'the mutual pursuit of peaceful coexistence as a deliberate and systematic policy of optimizing East-West collaboration' as 'quite another matter'. See his 'Genoa revisited: Russia and Coexistence' *Foreign Affairs* vol. 50, no. 3 (April 1972), p. 568.

[61] See *24th Congress of the CPSU*, pp. 35f. Cf. also G. A. Arbatov, 'A step serving the interests of peace', printed in the Soviet journal *USA*, Nov. 1971, reprinted in *Survival* Jan/Feb. 1972 p. 19, giving a full quote of the relevant passage in Brezhnev's report.

[62] *Declaration on Peace, Security and Cooperation in Europe*, adopted by the Political Consultative Committee of the Warsaw Treaty Member States at

their meeting in Prague, 25–26 January 1972, *Pravda*, 27 January 1972 and *Soviet News* no. 5624, 1 February 1972. The italics are mine.

[63] See Ernst Scholz, 'Politik der friedlichen Koexistenz von Nutzen für alle Völker' *Aussenpolitische Korrespondenz* no. 8, 23 February 1972. Cf. also Honecker's speech at Leipzig, 10 March 1972, in which he referred to the 'gesture of good-will' announced by the GDR on 23 February 1972 (see above, note 43) and asserted, 'Everyone has been able to convince himself once again that the Socialist Unity Party of Germany and our republic are in earnest in their support of the letter and spirit of the policy of peaceful coexistence ... For us, words and deeds are in conformity ...', *Foreign Affairs Bulletin* (GDR) no. 9, 23 March 1972.

[64] At the beginning of 1972 the East German authorities proclaimed 'the opening of the frontiers towards the socialist neighbour countries, Poland and Czechoslovakia'. The 5th Central Committee Plenum of the SED decided in early May 1972 to implement social security measures implying very substantial improvements. Cf. *Foreign Affairs Bulletin* (GDR) no. 14, 11 May 1972.

[65] See above, p. 62. In 1972 the East German campaign for the international recognition of the GDR focused on participation in the Stockholm Conference on the Human Environment and on membership in the UN and its specialised agencies.

4 The Formalisation of inter-German Relations

When, in the spring of 1972, the East-West package deal was validated, the formal relationship between the two German states had been left unsettled. Yet, a formalisation of these relations was necessary if the predictions of statesmen in East and West, that the negotiated agreements would usher in a new, mutually advantageous stage in intra-European affairs, were to be fulfilled. While the negotiations leading up to the agreement on traffic questions had enabled Bonn and East Berlin to regulate their relations to some extent,[1] a more definite clarification of the German situation was required if *les querelles allemandes* were not to bedevil impending East-West negotiations in a multilateral framework.[2] If, furthermore, it is true – as argued above – that the gradual opening toward the West on the part of the WTO countries, implicit in the concluded agreements, presupposed a further consolidation of the East German state and its government, then the participation of the GDR leadership in international negotiations on an equal and fully clarified legal basis was in the overall interest of East-West *détente* and *rapprochement*. At the Moscow summit meeting in May 1972 the leaders of the United States and the Soviet Union demonstrated their determination to pursue the search for accommodation and to enlarge the area of co-operation. Both German states had to adapt themselves to the requirements of this all-important trend in world politics.

1 Basic positions and interests of the two German governments

The negotiating positions of the two German governments with regard to the future of their mutual relations were to a large extent circumscribed and pre-determined by the preceding agreements between East and West. At the same time, however, these agreements, notably the Four Power accord on Berlin, failed to clarify fully some crucial issues that were of major importance for the future development of relations between the two German states. This was particularly true of the rights and responsibilities of the Victor Powers in Germany as a whole, and the way these applied to the GDR and East Berlin.

As far as Bonn was concerned, there was no reason to revise the line of policy set out in the twenty point programme that Mr. Brandt had put forward at the second German summit meeting in Kassel on 21 May 1970.[3] It aimed at ensuring progress towards a substantive normalisation of conditions in Germany parallel with the working out of ways of formalising inter-German relations. Developments since the Kassel meeting had shown that a policy based on this concept could lead to practical results: during 1971 and early 1972 improvements in the international standing of the GDR had been successfully traded for tangible improvements in contact and communication between the people of the two German states, and further progress along the same line appeared to be within reach.[4]

However, since Bonn was approaching a point in its *Deutschlandpolitik* where a full regulation of its relations with East Germany would become necessary, the conditions for formalisation that would be either desirable or acceptable had to be spelled out more explicitly. Two main preoccupations seem to have been in the minds of West Germany's policy makers at this juncture:

1) Since the East German leaders had tended to interpret the quadripartite agreement on Berlin in a restrictive manner, any accord with them regularising the general character of inter-German relations had to be accompanied by measures and provisions conducive to the implementation of the improvements in the position of West Berlin resulting from the letter and spirit of the Four Power agreement.

2) A treaty formalising the relations between the FRG and the GDR must not be allowed to jeopardise West Germany's long-term aspirations – which had been taken into account in the agreements with Moscow and Warsaw – for a qualitative transformation of conditions in Central Europe leading eventually to a situation in which the German people would be able to exercise its right of self-determination and, if it so wished, achieve national unity.

The first concern implied that the West German side was anxious to ensure that the maintenance and development of existing ties between the FRG and West Berlin, provided for in the quadripartite agreement, would be explicitly acknowledged and respected by East Germany. While, due to the prerogatives of the Four Powers, stipulations to that effect could hardly be part of a formal treaty between the two German states, it was essential that Bonn elicit guarantees from the East German side that the agreements between the FRG and the GDR on practical improvements in inter-German relations would also apply to West Berlin.

Three central concepts in the West German negotiating position were related to the long-term prospects for German unity and self-determination: firstly, the emphasis put on the continued validity of Four Power rights and responsibilities for Berlin and Germany as a whole; secondly, the insistence on 'the extraordinary situation of Germany and the Germans, who live in two states and yet are members of *one* nation'[5]; and thirdly, as a consequence of these circumstances, the contention that the 'special relations' between the two German states should be reflected in the appointment of 'plenipotentia-

74

ries of ministerial rank', rather than ambassadors to represent the respective governments in Bonn and East Berlin.[6]

Available evidence suggests that the East German leaders viewed an inter-German agreement formalising relations between the two states mainly from the vantage point of its effect on the international standing of the GDR and their own power position. They had always striven for the international recognition of the GDR as a measure conducive to consolidating both the political viability of the East German state and the rule of the SED in it. Ever since the signing of the quadripartite agreement on Berlin in September 1971, Mr. Honecker and his associates had sought to exploit the momentum created by that agreement for an improvement of the GDR's international status. Bonn's contention that the diplomatic recognition of East Germany by third states should be made dependent on an inter-German accord had been denounced as discriminatory and counter-productive. Yet, the performance of the SED during autumn 1971 and spring 1972 had shown that under certain conditions the East German leaders could be led to acquiesce in the gradual application of the much decried 'Scheel-doctrine'.

With the final validation of the East-West package deal in June 1972, however, the hopes of the East German leadership of achieving a break-through in international recognition without any major concessions to Bonn were given a new impetus. East Berlin was now trying to establish a kind of reverse connection, arguing that East German membership of the United Nations was liable to have a favourable effect on inter-German relations.[7] When, in early June 1972, Mr. Honecker commented on the ratification of Bonn's Eastern treaties, he emphasised the importance of the declaration of intent in the Moscow treaty (committing the parties to promoting the accession of both German states to the UN in acheiving 'a new relationship' between the GDR and the FRG.[8] A few weeks later the East German Foreign Minister, Mr. Winzer, spoke of a stage having been reached, at which the two German states' membership of the world organisation had 'not only become possible, but also urgently necessary.'[9]

If, as a result of the validation of the East-West package deal, the East German leaders had reason to expect an erosion of the 'Scheel-doctrine' and a concomitant strengthening of their negotiating position *vis-à-vis* Bonn,[10] other considerations were soon to counterbalance these factors. Discussions at a conference of the leaders of the WTO member states in the Crimea on 30–31 July 1972 apparently resulted in agreement on a general line of policy aimed at assisting West Germany's ruling SPD/FDP coalition in its domestic struggle against the conservative forces of the CDU/CSU. This in turn presupposed a forthcoming attitude on the part of the SED towards the Brandt/Scheel government in the negotiations about a regularisation of inter-German relations, since that issue was bound to play a significant role in the impending West German election campaign.[11] In its comments on the Crimean meeting the SED leadership used distinctly appreciative words about the role of the SPD/FDP government in bringing about a new situation in Europe, a pronouncement that was generally interpreted as a signal of its willingness to co-operate in achieving a speedy formalisation of inter-German relations.[12]

As East Berlin was preparing to regularise its relationship with Bonn, the following preoccupations seem to have dominated the thinking of Mr. Honecker and his associates:

1) The status of the German Democratic Republic as a sovereign and independent state had to be safeguarded in the agreement with Bonn.

2) Consequently, it was essential to avoid all formulas that could be interpreted as a limitation of East Germany's sovereign rights and to achieve a discontinuation of West German practices that were considered as discriminatory.

3) In spite of the mutual de-escalation of threatening political behaviour in East and West, the SED tended to view the very existence of a Western enclave in Berlin as a challenge to the viability and stability of the East German state. The closer the ties between the FRG and West Berlin, the greater the perceived challenge. An agreement with Bonn, therefore, must at least not strengthen these ties.

4) Any further steps in the direction of increased human contact and freer communication between the GDR and the FRG resulting from an inter-German agreement had to be kept within distinct limits and be fully controllable by East German authorities.

Among the pronouncements and measures reflecting these East German concerns some were especially revealing. Thus, Mr. Honecker was at pains to denounce all attempts at providing the relations between the two German states with an 'intra-German' label, viewing this as an encroachment on East German sovereignty and therefore totally unacceptable.[13] Foreign Minister Winzer went a step further when, a few weeks later, he not only described the concept of the unity of the German nation as being without any foundation, but also challenged the continued validity of Four Power rights in Germany.[14] With respect to Berlin, the performance of the SED during the summer of 1972 made it abundantly clear that, in their practical application of the quadripartite agreement, the East German leaders were attempting to establish the rule – contravening the spirit of the agreement – that those ties between West Berlin and the FRG that had not been explicitly sanctioned were in fact forbidden. Such an interpretation of the Berlin agreement would have made mockery of the provision allowing ties between West Berlin and West Germany not only to be maintained but also developed.[15] Finally, with regard to contact and communication between the two German states, the

East German authorities had, ever since 1970, been perfecting the physical barrier along the inter-German border. These efforts were speeded up in spring 1971 and again in summer 1972, thereby creating a situation which appeared paradoxical at first glance only of the East German political opening towards the West being counterbalanced by administrative and technical measures aimed at further containing the possibilities of unauthorised contact and communication with West Germany.[16]

2 The road to the Basic Treaty

While the *formal* negotiations between State Secretaries Egon Bahr and Michael Kohl leading up to the completion of a treaty on the basis of relations between the two German states took less than three months, some of the main issues with which they had had to deal had been the subject of intensive and prolonged talks over a much longer period. Since at least autumn 1971 the representatives of the FRG and the GDR had, in their mutual exchanges, to a large extent occupied themselves with the basic character of inter-German relations. During the ensuing weeks and months they concentrated on two main subjects, namely transit to West Berlin and the regulation of inter-German traffic. But in the course of these negotiations a solid groundwork had been laid facilitating the subsequent tackling of wider questions of principle.[17] This fact was reflected in the joint statement announcing, on 15 June 1972, the initiation of preparatory talks between Messrs. Bahr and Kohl on the formalisation of FRG-GDR relations. The formula used there to describe the subject matter of the new round of *pourparlers* was taken from the preamble of the newly concluded treaty on traffic questions, and thus referred to 'the establishment of normal good-neighbourly relations customary between states that were independent of each other'.[18]

The first stage of these exchanges was completed by the end of June 1972. After three meetings the rough outlines of a treaty, comprising a preamble and nine substantive articles, had been worked out, the basis being a draft put forward originally by the East German side.[19] This suggests that it had been possible to identify comparatively quickly the main controversial issues around which the substantive negotiations would primarily revolve. After the summer recess both German governments were therefore in a position to authorise their representatives to enter into formal negotiations. In its decision to that effect the West German Cabinet emphasised the following guidelines for these negotiations: firstly, to promote the cohesion of the German nation; secondly, not to impede German reunification; and thirdly, to achieve a maximum of practical co-operation between the two states in Germany.[20]

After two sessions of the negotiating teams in August 1972 the seemingly incompatible positions of the two sides were exposed in public. East Germany, at that juncture, insisted on normal relations *under international law* and consequently on the exchange of ambassadors between Bonn and East Berlin. The West German leaders, on the other hand, showed no inclination to accept *diplomatic* relations between the FRG and the GDR, since they continued to claim that a formalisation of relations with East Berlin must somehow reflect the special situation prevailing in Germany.[21] The available evidence does not permit us to reconstruct the ensuing tug-of-war in all its details. It is, however, possible to illustrate the gradual convergence of the two sides' positions on some of the central issues, and to attempt to relate these developments to international events and their repercussions on the German scene.

To judge from pronouncements and hints from both sides, their intensive negotiations during September and October narrowed the gap between the respective stands but produced no 'breakthrough'. The East Germans soon ceased to talk about an exchange of ambassadors with Bonn and used other formulas to describe the nature of their future relations with the Federal Republic. By the end of October, it had become clear that the GDR no longer insisted on West German recognition on the basis of international law and was willing to accept that inter-German relations would distinguish themselves from those the two German states entertained with third countries.[22] On other controversial issues, however, the two sides were still quite far apart.

International developments during the preceding weeks had brought advantages to both German states. East Germany had been able to register significant successes with regard to its international standing: in early September Finland had become the first non-Communist state in Europe to announce its intention of establishing diplomatic relations with East Berlin; and a few weeks later India formally recognised the GDR.[23] These events encouraged the East German leaders to redouble their efforts at weakening the link established by Bonn between UN membership of the German states and an inter-German agreement. [24] In the meantime, however, the West German contention had not only been favourably received by the new Secretary General of the United Nations[25], but supported by the United States as well. The American government, during informal consultations among the Four Powers, had made it clear that it would not consent to East German membership of the United Nations unless the GDR explicitly acknowledged the rights and responsibilities of the Four Powers in Germany. There could, furthermore, be no doubt that the Soviet Union, too, wished to see these rights preserved.[26]

The mutual interest of the super-powers in stabilising and pacifying conditions in Europe manifested itself during the visit to Moscow, between 10 and 14 September 1972, of Mr. Henry Kissinger, Special Adviser to President Nixon. His conversations with the Soviet leaders resulted in an agreement on parallel procedures with regard to the preparations for a CSCE and preliminary talks on Mutual Balanced Force Reductions (MBFR). Against the background of this agreement it now appeared most likely that the proposed multilateral consultations in preparation for a CSCE would start on 22 November 1972 as suggested by the Finnish government. Bonn had a vested interest in achieving an agreement with East Berlin prior to that date, since its negotiating position was expected to deteriorate once East Germany had taken part in multilateral diplomatic negotiations on an equal footing with other states.[27] On the other hand, it was plausible to assume that the Soviet Union would not wish to see the multilateral talks at Helsinki complicated by unsettled inter-German issues, and that Moscow was therefore anxious to promote an agreement between Bonn and East Berlin before 22 November 1972.

Some of the advantages that West Germany could derive from international developments during the early autumn of 1972 were the results of its own diplomatic efforts. Two events were of particular significance: the establishment of diplomatic relations with Peking, and the consultations of Mr. Bahr with the Soviet leaders during his visit to Moscow on 8–10 October 1972. The latter step was immediately relevant to the negotiations with East Berlin, since it cleared the way for the adoption of a formula reconfirming the continued validity of the rights and responsibilities of the former Victor Powers in Germany. This formula had to be accepted by the UN Security Council in order to make it possible for the two German states to become members of the world organisation. Since the Peking government was now representing China in the Security Council, its acquiescence to the proposed formula was essential for the successful implementation of a policy of inter-German normalisation, whose calculated consequence it was to enable both German states to participate in the work of the United Nations.

The Chinese leaders had previously denounced the Moscow treaty of 1970 and subsequent East-West agreements as instances of collusion between imperialists and revisionists aimed against the true interests of the peoples concerned. However, as a consequence of the reorientation of China's international policies since 1971, Peking was now prepared to acquiesce in the results of the East-West negotiations of 1970–72. In connection with the establishment of diplomatic relations between Peking and Bonn, China's Prime Minister Mr. Chou En-lai declared that his country would support the application of the two German states for UN membership. When he made that statement the Chinese leader was well aware of the fact that the application would be provided with a rider on the continued validity of the rights and responsibilities of the Four Powers.[28]

Mr. Bahr's visit to Moscow was arranged at the initiative of the West German side and occurred at a moment when the inter-German negotiations had entered a very difficult stage. Mr. Bahr was at pains to avoid creating the impression that he was trying to enlist Moscow's help to break a deadlock in the talks with East Berlin[29]; but there could be no doubt that an exchange of views at that juncture between the Soviet leaders and the West German chief negotiator, known to enjoy their full confidence, was liable to have a major impact on the subsequent course of events. The talks, formally part of the regular Soviet-West German consultations agreed upon at the Oreanda meeting in September 1971, necessarily had the character of a *tour d'horizon*. However, Messrs Bahr and Gromyko confirmed afterwards that they included a thorough discussion of the ways of reconfirming the rights and responsibilities of the Four Powers in Germany.[30]

Soviet performance in the latter part of October suggests that Mr. Bahr's personal representations in Moscow had not been in vain. On 23 October 1972 the Soviet Union entered into formal talks with the United States, Britain and France on the possibility of the GDR and the FRG becoming members of the United Nations. With this Moscow implicitly acknowledged the existence of Four Power rights and reponsibilities not only with regard to Berlin, where they had been reconfirmed through the quadripartite agreement, but also for Germany as a whole.[31]

By the end of October the overall political situation gave rise to the expectation that, in spite of serious remaining differences, Bonn and East Berlin would exert themselves to conclude their negotiations prior to the start of multilateral talks in Helsinki and also before the impending general elections in West Germany on 19 November 1972. While both sides had officially denied that the latter date was of any significance for the inter-German negotiations, the very uncertainty of the election outcome was liable to create powerful incentives for both German governments to reach an agreement before the West German citizens had cast their votes.

It was understandable that the SPD/FDP government should wish to complete its *Ostpolitik* with an inter-German agreement before the election. This would tend to refocus public attention on an issue from which the government coalition could legitimately expect to derive political benefit. Furthermore, since the policy-making group in Bonn seemed genuinely convinced that it was both in the short-term and long-term interest of the German people to conclude this agreement, and since it had doubts of whether a CDU/CSU government would be in a position to negotiate *any* agreement with East Berlin in the foreseeable future, Mr. Brandt and his associates were, it appears, inclined to strike a bargain with the GDR before 19 November 1972, *provided* the essential conditions stipulated in the guidelines for Mr. Bahr were fulfilled. In this way a situation could be created which while not *legally* binding on any future West German government – since it was not expected that a treaty with the GDR would be *signed* before election day – would nevertheless be virtually irreversible from a *political* viewpoint. Only in the unlikely event of a defeat of the governing coalition being shown conclusively to be the voters' negative verdict on the deal with East Berlin, could a new government reverse such a situation.

The East German side, on the other hand, must have been aware that, while the momentum behind the overall trend towards East-West *détente* and co-operation might be somewhat delayed by a change of government in Bonn, it was likely to reassert itself in the long run irrespective of the election outcome in West Germany. If the SED leadership did not conclude an agreement with Bonn before the election, it could in the event of a CSU/CDU victory sooner or later expect new difficulties with its allies on account of East German 'obstruction' of the general policy line of the WTO member states towards the West. West Germany was likely to find itself in a similar situation *vis-à-vis its* allies after a change of government in Bonn. Thus, it would seem both German governments had tangible reasons to do their utmost in order to come to terms with each other prior to November 19, 1972.

In the final stage of the inter-German negotiations one of the main contested issues was the question of how, if at all, Bonn's long-term aspiration for ensuring the self-determination and national unity of all Germans could be accommodated in a treaty with the GDR without implicitly jeopardising the latter's independent and equal status. On 12 October 1972 Mr. Brandt had asserted publicly that his government would sign a treaty with East Germany only if this did not require a change in the West German constitution (the *Grundgesetz*).[32] Since the preamble of the latter committed the government in Bonn to striving for the self-determination and unification of the whole German people, the Chancellor's pronouncement must have removed any remaining doubts on the East German side about the necessity of finding *some* formula that would eliminate the risk of the Brandt/Scheel government's being susceptible to the charge of acting in contradiction with the letter and/or spirit of the *Grundgesetz*. That this issue was the main bone of contention is borne out by a statement of Mr. Bahr on 26 October 1972. Denying rumours that a compromise formula had been found, he stressed that had this been the case there would indeed be reason to speak of a 'breakthrough' in the negotiations. The GDR, Mr. Bahr claimed on that occasion, was still not prepared to make any reference whatsoever to the national question in a treaty with Bonn.[33] Within ten days, however, agreement was reached on a mutually acceptable compromise.

The other major issue over which the two German negotiating teams fought until the very end was the question how the provisions of an inter-German treaty were to be related to West Berlin. The insistence of the West German representative that this issue must not be side-stepped was due in part at least to the fact that the Four Power accord on Berlin had contained no provisions about the way in which future agreements between the two German states were to affect West Berlin. A failure to tackle this issue in connection with a treaty aimed at regularising inter-German relations could therefore be interpreted as West German acquiescence in a *de facto* loosening of ties between the FRG and West Berlin. In view of the East German inclination to interpret the quadripartite agreement in a restrictive manner, any such lacunae were likely to be exploited by the GDR leaders to the full. No wonder, then, that a critical situation seemed to arise at the beginning of the very last round of negotiations, which started on 2 November 1972. The East German side at first refused to include any provisions about West Berlin in the agreement with the FRG. However, in the course of intensive negotiations in East Berlin on 3 and 4 November, which were interrupted at times to enable Mr. Bahr to consult both with Bonn and with the Western ambassadors, simultaneously engaged in talks with the Soviet Union on a Four Power declaration, a solution acceptable to both sides was at last found.[34]

In the negotiations of the Four Powers the efforts of the Western side to incorporate some reference to Germany as a whole in the proposed declaration met with determined Soviet resistance. Here too a compromise formula was eventually adopted, taking into account the preoccupation of the SED leadership with safeguarding East Germany's sovereignty. At the same time, the reconfirmation of the rights and responsibilities of the Four Powers in connection with the impending accession of both German states to the United Nations, also satisfied West German demands.[35] On 6 November, the texts of the inter-German treaty and accompanying documents could be finalised, and, after having been approved by the two governments, they were initialled by Messrs. Bahr and Kohl on 8 November 1972.

When, eleven days later the SPD/FDP coalition won a decisive victory in the West German general election, it became clear that the Basic Treaty would come into force and a formalisation of inter-German relations be accomplished. The essence of the new *Ostpolitik*, initiated by the Brandt/Scheel government in 1969, had thus been realised in accordance with the original policy concept.

3 The formal basis for normalisation and co–operation

The essence of the Basic Treaty[36] was that it codified a *modus vivendi* between the two German states on the basis of the existing situation. Since the latter was, to say the least, complex, the treaty necessarily constituted a highly complicated structure of interlocking provisions and agreements. With regard to all major contested points, the formulations and arrangements finally agreed upon reflected compromises between the conflicting preoccupations of the two sides: on the one hand Bonn's long-term aspiration of keeping the option of German unity open and its short-term goal of ensuring maximum human contact and exchange in divided Germany; on the other hand East Berlin's wish to demonstrate the independence and equality of the GDR and to safeguard and consolidate the distinctiveness and viability of its political and social order. These objectives were to a large extent incompatible. Consequently, an agreement between the parties aimed at formalising and normalising their relations inevitably implied that on central issues there could be no more than a mutual registering of, and reciprocal acquiescence in, the respective positions of the two sides.

The main yardstick for West German concessions on questions of status were the provisions made in the preamble of the *Grundgesetz*, which committed the whole German people, and consequently the government in Bonn, to strive for German unity and self-determination. The need for conformity with these constitutional stipulations was satisfied in the Basic Treaty. While its preamble did not speak of the continued existence of *one* German nation, as originally envisaged by Bonn, it explicitly acknowledged the existence of 'the national question', even though it registered the differing views of the two German states on that fundamental issue. The treaty also recognised the continued validity of the rights and responsibilities of the Four Powers. This was ensured implicitly in Article 9 and explicitly in the correspondence to take place between the two sides in connection with the signing of the treaty.[37] The latter step implied that the GDR for the first time legally recognised the prerogatives of the Four Powers (the United States, the Soviet Union, Britain and France) in Germany as a whole.

The acknowledgment of this Four Power 'roof' in the Basic Treaty amounted to the preservation of a residual legal element of German unity, which, in addition to the references to 'the national question', was essential if the risk of complications in connection with the ratification of the treaty by the West German parliament were to be eliminated. A final guarantee of the compatibility between the treaty and the prescriptions of the *Grundgesetz* was created through an arrangement by which the West German government – as in the case of the Moscow treaty – would address to the GDR a 'letter on German unity' which East Berlin would accept unreservedly.[38]

As for the East German side, which was anxious to improve its status *vis-à-vis* West Germany, the limit of any concessions was constituted by the need to avoid formulations that could be construed as an infringement of the independence and autonomy of the GDR. The Basic Treaty did not contain any stipulation by which the FRG explicitly recognised the sovereignty of the GDR, since this would have conflicted with the preservation of a residual legal element of German unity in the form of Four Power rights.

Yet, formulations were to be found in Article 6 by which East Germany's urgent demand for an explicit West German acknowledgment of its autonomy and independence could be satisfied. In addition, Article 4 implied a formal and definite abrogation of earlier West German claims of 'sole representation': both states would henceforth proceed on the assumption that neither of them could represent the other in the international sphere or act on its behalf. Both the preamble and Article 2 contained a statement of aims and principles, including the sovereign equality and territorial integrity of all states, which were liable to gratify the East German side.[39] Finally, Article 3 reaffirmed the present and future inviolability of the frontier between the two German states and included an explicit mutual undertaking to respect each other's territorial integrity.

While these provisions met basic concerns on the part of the GDR leadership, the special nature of future inter-German relations was nevertheless safeguarded in the agreement. Article 8 stipulated that the two states were to exchange *permanent missions*, not ambassadors, as is customary in diplomatic relations. Furthermore, inter-German trade was to develop on the basis of existing arrangements, which implied that the GDR was not treated by the FRG as a foreign country and thus enjoyed the advantages of belonging to the Customs Union of the EEC.[40]

If the Basic Treaty represented a fair compromise on fundamental questions of status, the inclusion of West Berlin in the agreement was a substantive success for the West German side, although the settlement of this issue also took into account East German interests and sensitivities. According to identical statements to be made, on signing the treaty, by both sides, the extension of future practical and humanitarian agreements between the FRG and the GDR could be agreed upon in conformity with the quadripartite agreement. In addition, the permanent mission of the FRG was to represent the interests of West Berlin, while arrangements between the GDR and the *Senat* of West Berlin would remain unaffected.

While the formal regularisation of inter-German relations was the main concern of the Basic Treaty, further measures of substantive normalisation were also provided by the agreement. The most spectacular novelty here was the possibility it opened up for West German citizens living in 56 districts near the border to visit adjacent areas on the East German side. This arrangement was meant to enable more than 6 million people in the Federal Republic to spend up to 30 days per year in nearby parts of East Germany, even if the purpose was only tourism. Other practical improvements included the opening of further border crossings, more liberal regulations aiming at the unification of families, the facilitation of non-commercial goods traffic and other amendments of existing practices.[41]

The limited opening of the GDR implied in these stipulations was a rather one-sided affair, since the new opportunities for East Germans to visit the Federal Republic were minimal. Yet, there was reason to expect that, if they were implemented in accordance with the letter and spirit of the agreement, the increase in person-to-person contact across the inter-German boundary would eventually create a distinctly new situation despite the continued existence, and even perfection, of the physical barrier along that border line.

The treaty on the basis of relations between the two German states signified the end of a period of hostile confrontation in the heart of Europe. In this sense it was the missing link in the attempts of the super-powers and their main allies to achieve a measure of mutual accommodation. 'We have organized coexistence *[das Nebeneinander]*; it remains for us to learn co-operation *[das Miteinander]*' Mr. Brandt said on the occasion of the conclusion of the inter-German negotiations.[42] The extent to which the inter-German agreement will create a period of co-operation between the FRG and the GDR depends, of course, on the way in which it is implemented and on the wider process of an intensified East-West interaction in Europe.

Notes

[1] In the preamble of the inter-German traffic agreement the two sides committed themselves to the goal of striving for 'normal, good-neighbourly relations..., as are customary among states independent of each other.' See *Treaty between the German Democratic Republic and the Federal Republic of Germany on Questions Relating to Traffic*, initialled on 12 May and signed on 26 May 1972; unofficial East German translation (Dresden, Verlag Zeit im Bild) p. 5.

[2] At a meeting in Bonn on 30–31 May 1972, the members of the Atlantic Alliance had agreed to enter into multilateral negotiations for the preparation of a CSCE. See communiqué from the ministerial session of the North Atlantic Council 30–31 May 1972; NATO Press Release MI(72) 7, 31 May 1972.

[3] See *Kassel May 21, 1970. A Documentation* pp. 84ff.

[4] Apart from the opening of telephone lines between East and West Berlin the main steps to be mentioned in this connection were the postal agreement of 30 September 1971; the agreement on transit traffic to West Berlin that came into force in early June 1972 as part of the quadripartite accord; and the general agreement on inter-German traffic signed on 26 May 1972. Cf. above, Chapter 2, p.46 and Chapter 3, p. 63.

[5] Quotation from point 10 in the 20 point programme presented by the West German side at the Kassel Meeting; cf. *Kassel May 21, 1970. A Documentation* p. 85.

[6] Cf. point 19, *ibid.*, p. 86. For a perceptive analysis of the West German position on the eve of the start of substantive inter-German negotiations about a *Grundvertrag* see Theo Sommer, 'Deutschlandpolitik – die letzte Etappe' *Die Zeit*, 11 August 1972.

[7] It can be assumed with some confidence that the East German leaders were not unaware of the existence of a faction in the policy-making group in Bonn, who had argued all along that the participation of the GDR in international life on a basis of full equality was more likely to produce a forthcoming East German attitude on inter-German relations than the strict application of the 'Scheel-doctrine'.

[8] See Honecker's interview with ADN on 6 June 1972, *Neues Deutschland*, 7 June 1972.

[9] Cf. Winzer's interview with ADN on 2 July 1972, *Aussenpolitische Korrespondenz* no. 27, 5 July 1972.

[10] At the beginning of 1972 India had committed herself to postponing the establishment of diplomatic relations with the GDR until after the ratification of Bonn's Eastern treaties. The Indian recognition of East Germany was therefore impending. On 10 July 1972 Finland renewed an earlier proposal to establish diplomatic relations with both German states. And on 12 July 1972 agreement was reached between Switzerland and the GDR on the exchange of trade missions.

[11] On 24 June 1972 Chancellor Brandt had announced the decision of the government coalition SPD/FDP to seek new elections to the *Bundestag* by November 1972 in order to break the political impasse in the FRG resulting from the absence of a dependable parliamentary majority.

[12] See declaration issued by the Politbureau of the SED on 2 August 1972, *Neues Deutschland* 3 August 1972; for a similar statement by the Politbureau of the CPSU, published on 6 August 1972, which did not mention West Germany explicitly but only referred to 'the constructive attitudes of other countries concerned', see *Soviet News* no. 5650, 8 August 1972. Cf. also Joachim Nawrocki, 'Erich Honecker muss einlenken' *Die Zeit* 11 August 1972.

[13] See Honecker's ADN interview on 6 June 1972, cf. note 8 above.

[14] See Otto Winzer, 'Zu einigen aktuellen Problemen im Zusammenhang mit dem Meinungsaustausch zwischen der DDR und der BRD' *Horizont* no. 28/1972. This is based on a lecture he delivered on 23 June 1972.

[15] See *The Quadripartite Agreement [on Berlin] of Sept. 3, 1971*, Annex II, pp. 16ff; cf. also J. Nawrocki, 'Querschüsse gegen Berlin' *Die Zeit*, 22 September 1972.

[16] See declaration of Mr. Schmülling, representative of the West German Ministry of the Interior at a press conference given by Mr. Bahr on 19 October 1972, as paraphrased in *Süddeutsche Zeitung* 20–21 October 1972.

Cf. also Karl-Heinz Janssen, '"Mordmaschine" oder "moderne Grenze"?' *Die Zeit* 27 October 1972.

[17] Cf. statement by Mr. Bahr at a press conference on 26 May 1972 after the signing of the inter-German traffic agreement, reprinted in *Neues Deutschland*, 27 May 1972.

[18] Joint statement issued by the representatives of the FRG and the GDR on 15 June 1972, *Neues Deutschland*, 16 June 1972.

[19] The fact the Mr. Kohl put forward a first draft for the proposed treaty is borne out by an official East German statement issued on the occasion of the initialling of the Basic Treaty on 8 November 1972. See ADN statement published in *Aussenpolitische Korrespondenz*, Sonderausgabe, 9 November 1972. Cf. also Kohl's statement in a Hungarian television programme on 2 July 1972, where he stressed that the East German side had put 'concrete proposals on the negotiating table' *ibid.* no. 28, 12 July 1972. The alleged East German draft treaty published by the West German weekly *Quick* shortly before the conclusion of the negotiations probably represented an early, though not the first, East German proposal. Cf. *Quick* no. 44, 25 October 1972.

[20] Cf. statement by State Secretary Conrad Ahlers on 9 August 1972, paraphrasing the main contents of the Cabinet decision. *Süddeutsche Zeitung*, 10 August 1972.

[21] The East German position was at that time, publicly expounded by Mr. Kohl in an interview with West German television on 31 August 1972. For the text see *Aussenpolitische Korrespondenz* no. 36, 6 September 1972. The West German stand was clarified by Mr. Bahr in a similar interview on the same day.

[22] In the report of the Politbureau delivered by Mr. Werner Lamberz at the 7th Plenary session of the Central Committee of the SED on 12 October 1972, it was emphasised that a treaty with the FRG 'must take into account the facts of international law' (*muss den völkerrechtlichen Gegebenheiten Rechnung tragen*), a formula that was not incompatible with the West German position. See *Aussenpolitische Korrespondenz* no. 41/42, 18 October 1972. In an interview on 26 October 1972 Mr. Kohl indicated that the relations between the two German states must be in accordance with the goals and principles of the UN but did not repeat earlier explicit demands for diplomatic recognition by the FRG. This was confirmed by Mr. Bahr in an interview with *Flensburger Tageblatt* on 26 October 1972, in which he asserted that this problem was now 'aus der Welt'. Cf. report in *Süddeutsche Zeitung* 27 October 1972.

[23] For a joint statement announcing the successful conclusion of negotiations on the establishment of diplomatic relations between the GDR and Finland on 6 September 1972, see *Aussenpolitische Korrespondenz* no. 37, 13

September 1972. The establishment of diplomatic relations with India was officially announced on 8 October 1972. See *ibid.* no. 41/42, 18 October 1972.

24 See, for example, the East German Deputy Foreign Minister, Mr. Ewaldt Moldt's, interview with 'a leading French newspaper' on 6 October 1972, reprinted in *Aussenpolitische Korrespondenz* no. 41/42, 18 October 1972.

25 While Mr. Waldheim had repeatedly stressed the urgency of East and West German membership in the UN he is reported as expressing agreement with Bonn's position that a clarification of inter-German relations must precede the accession of both German states to the UN. See State Secretary Ahler's declaration about a meeting between Messrs. Brandt and Waldheim in Munich on 26 August 1972, *Süddeutsche Zeitung*, 28 August 1972.

26 On the American position cf. for example a declaration by Mr. Walter Stoessel, head of the European division in the Department of State, at a meeting with 'overseas writers' in Washington on 5 October 1972; as reported in *Süddeutsche Zeitung*, 6 October 1972. See also Willi Kinnigkeit, 'Die internationale Aufwertung der DDR durch Indien' *ibid.*, 9 October 1972. Moscow's interest in stressing the continued validity of Four Power rights in the whole of Germany can be deduced from the fact that, when on 27 July 1972 Mr. Honecker received the new commander of Soviet forces in the GDR, his official title was given as 'supreme commander of the group of Soviet forces in Germany' and a note to that effect was published on the first page of *Neues Deutschland* (28 July 1972). Previously East German sources had often referred to the Soviet troops as 'forces temporarily stationed in the GDR'.

27 Mr. Bahr had stated publicly that the convening of a CSCE could not be made dependent on the conclusion of an inter-German treaty. The view that West Germany's negotiating position *vis-à-vis* the GDR would deteriorate once multilateral preparations for the CSCE had started was a logical consequence of this stand. See Mr. Bahr's declaration in Moscow on 9 October 1972, as reported by J. Riedmiller in *Süddeutsche Zeitung*, 10 October 1972. Cf. also J. Nawrocki, 'Deutschland – ein allierter Vorbehalt?' *Die Zeit* 27 October 1972.

28 See Foreign Minister Walter Scheel's interview with *Deutschlandfunk* on 15 October 1972, *Bulletin* no. 144, 17 October 1972.

29 See Bahr's declarations prior to his departure for, and immediately after his arrival in, Moscow on 8 October 1972, as reported in *Suddeutsche Zeitung* 9 October 1972.

30 Cf. declarations by Bahr and Gromyko on 10 October 1972; paraphrased in *Süddeutsche Zeitung* 11 October 1972.

31 Cf. declaration on the Four Power talks published in *Soviet News* no. 5663, 14 November 1972.

[32] See speech by Mr. Brandt in *Ausserordentlicher Parteitag der SPD, 12.–13. Oktober 1972. Unkorrigiertes Protokoll, 12. Oktober 1972*, p. 62.

[33] Statement by Mr. Bahr on 26 October 1972, reported in *Süddeutsche Zeitung*, 27 October 1972.

[34] See *ibid.*, 3, 4/5 and 6 November 1972; cf. also *Frankfurter Allgemeine Zeitung*, 9 November 1972.

[35] For the text of the Four Power declaration, which was published on 9 November 1972, see *Soviet News* no. 5663, 14 November 1972.

[36] The official name of the agreement is *Treaty on the Basis of Relations between the Federal Republic of Germany and the German Democratic Republic*. In the West it is generally referred to as the *Basic Treaty*. For an English translation of the treaty see *The Bulletin* (published by the Press and Information Office of the Government of the FGR), vol. 20, no. 38, November 1972; also *Survival* January–February 1973, 31ff.

[37] See *ibid.*, pp. 294 and 297.

[38] See 'Hinweis betr. Schreiben an die DDR zur nationalen Frage' *Vertrag über die Grundlagen der Beziehungen zwischen der BRD und der DDR*, p. 50.

[39] The importance of these principles to the East German side is borne out by Mr. Kohl's statement in connection with the initialling of the treaty and by an official East German pronouncement issued on 9 November 1972. Cf. *Aussenpolitische Korrespondenz*, Sonderausgabe, 9 November 1972, pp. ii and vii.

[40] See Supplementary Protocol, Section II, Point 1, *Vertrag über die Grundlagen...*, p. 12.

[41] The main principles for measures of practical normalisation were stated in Article 7 of the Basic Treaty. Detailed stipulations were contained in the Supplementary Protocol and an exchange of letters between Messrs. Bahr and Kohl. See *Vertag über die Grundlagen...*, pp. 10, 19–29.

[42] See *Bulletin* no. 155, 8 November 1972.

5 Germany and the Future of East-West Relations in Europe

The fundamental challenge confronting the European nations of East and West since the new stage of their mutual relationships opened up in 1972 is to accomplish the transition from *accommodation* to *co-operation*. The human and material resources that could be released through the elimination of hostile confrontation and the extension of East-West co-operation are substantial indeed. Since the global imperatives of the 1970s and 1980s – the effective fight against world poverty and pollution as well as the curtailment of the arms race – call for a major reallocation of resources, the challenge before East and West in Europe also implies concerted efforts to bring about a reorientation of national concerns that would make such reallocation politically feasible. Viewed in a global context, it is therefore not enough for the European nations to institute mutually advantageous collaboration, however worthwhile and necessary this may appear. They must also direct their common efforts towards the solution of extra-European and global problems which are apt to affect the well-being of *all* people in a shrinking world.

Will the European nations meet this challenge? An attempt to answer that question in a comprehensive fashion is beyond the scope of the present investigation. What it is proposed to do in this concluding chapter is to discuss some crucial factors and current trends that are likely to determine the prospects for a successful transition to a period in the relations between Eastern and Western Europe that could rightly deserve to be called an era of co-operation. In so doing we shall at the same time identify necessary requirements for the kind of reorientation in the outlook and attitudes of ruling elites in East and West that would enable the Old Continent to play its proper part in meeting the global challenges of the last decades of the 20th century.

1 The results of accommodation

Speculations about future East-West relations in Europe must start with a brief assessment of what has been achieved. The crucial aspect of the East-West package deal resulting from the negotiations of 1970–71 was the fact that it represented a compromise implying genuine accommodation. The essential *quid pro quo* between East and West involved the mutual abandon-ment of political postures that had challenged the stability of social and political structures on the other side of the dividing line. Since these chal-lenges had previously been exploited for the manipulation of threat percep-tions, their elimination served to promote one of the fundamental premises of security and co-operation in Europe: the growing confidence of ruling elites and their constituents that force would not be used by any party to impose a preferred solution. The crucial question, then, is how far it will be possible to extirpate the remaining fears on both sides, to explore new oppor-tunities for fruitful East-West collaboration and yet avoid creating new instabilities and uncertainties which could bring the whole process of *détente* to a standstill.

The sustained evolution of mutual trust as a necessary precondition for co-operation is dependent not only on the political and military postures of the main actors but also on their assessment of the options of potential opponents and the way in which these are likely to be affected by trends in international politics. Ultimately, therefore, the potentialities opening up in the new stage of East-West relations in Europe may well depend on the way ruling elites in East and West view the effect of the recent agreements on the constraints and opportunities determining their future policy choices. While it is impossible to ascertain these views with any degree of precision and reliability, some reasonable assumptions can be derived from the deal itself.

As for the Soviet Union, it should be obvious that, in so far as its potential for generating tension in and around Berlin is a function of the Western enclave's exposed position, its capacity in that respect has not been signifi-cantly diminished. Nevertheless, Moscow's freedom of action has been dis-tinctly circumscribed. This is primarily due to the basic nature of the American-Soviet relationship that has developed in the present era, a rela-tionship which has often been characterised as one of limited hostility or a partnership of adversaries. It is the element of partnership in the relations of the super-powers that requires a certain amount of predictability and con-sistency in the attitudes of Moscow and Washington towards each other. As long as there was no formal agreement on Berlin the Soviet leadership could utilise its physical control over the access routes to West Berlin to put pres-sure on the Western powers and exploit differences between them, while retaining a sufficiently credible standing with Washington to continue the super-power dialogue and thus keep global competition with the United States within manageable bounds. After the Berlin agreement a balancing act of this kind has become virtually impossible. Furthermore, by virtue of its very existence, the Four Power accord makes it more difficult for Moscow to generate a crisis in Berlin, since to do so must henceforth involve breaking an international treaty of major significance.

Another important consequence of the East-West package deal, already referred to, is the elimination of the West German bogey as an instrument of Soviet policy both at home and abroad. This was undoubtedly necessary if Moscow wished to utilise its opportunities for closer political and economic co-operation with the Federal Republic. But this switch of attitudes compounds the old Soviet dilemma of managing *détente* with the West in such a way that destabilising repercussions in Eastern Europe could be avoided or at least minimised.

Most significantly, however, the East-West deal had for the first time enabled Moscow to concentrate on the stabilisation of conditions in Eastern Europe without simultaneously challenging the present arrangement of forces in the West. As long as Bonn did not accept the status quo in Central and Eastern Europe the Soviet Union was almost inevitably induced to establish a close link between its two major foreign policy goals in Europe, *consolidation* in the East and *fragmentation* in the West; only by breaking 'the Washington-Bonn axis' could Moscow hope to eliminate the threat to its empire that was purported to stem from the dangerous combination of a dissatisfied West Germany backed by the nuclear might of the American super-power. Once the Federal Republic accepted the prevailing territorial and political conditions in the Soviet realm – although with a view to changing them peacefully in the long run – the Soviet leadership had at least the opportunity of decoupling the two major goals of its European policy. That the Soviet Union now has the option of pursung a policy of consolidating the *status quo only* does not imply that it cannot continue to strive for the attainment of a *status quo plus* situation in Europe, giving Moscow increased leverage in its western part. Indeed, since the latter goal need no longer be sought by means that imply a direct challenge to existing Western institutions, Soviet policy in this direction could become more successful.

The pacification of Central Europe achieved in 1972 cleared the way for multilateral negotiations on the limitation of forces and armaments in Europe as well as on the extension of East-West trade and co-operation. This in turn provided an occasion and reason for intensified consultation and closer co-ordination of policy on East-West issues within both the military alliances in Europe and the states belonging to, or wishing to become members of, the European Community. For the United States the most important aspect of the East-West package deal was undoubtedly the fact that it reduced the likelihood of major international crises and, ultimately, an armed confrontation in one of the most fervently contested areas of world politics. While this may eventually enable Washington to reduce its military forces in Europe, one should not overlook the fact that the Four Power agreement on Berlin tends to stabilise the American position both there and in Europe generally.[1]

Since a combination of instability and high stakes continues to character-ise the inter-German situation, developments on the German scene are likely to remain the focal point of East-West relations in Europe. It seems justified, therefore, to devote special attention to the constraints and opportunities likely to determine the perceived options of policy makers in Bonn and East Berlin.

In view of the polarisation of the main political forces in West Germany it is important to recognise that the accommodation with the East achieved by 1972 represents an irreversible fact in the eyes of virtually all responsible politicians in the FRG. It can therefore be assumed with confidence that whatever the party affiliations of future West German governments, their assessment of the requirements and opportunities in the realm of East-West relations will take this accord as a foundation for future policy. The setting of West German *Ostpolitik* after the East-West agreements will be viewed similarly by both major political parties in the FRG in another sense too, for the interdependence of domestic pressures and external opportunities, as well as Western cohesion and East-West *détente*, is apt to be a source of continued, if not growing concern to Bonn.

The negotiations of 1970–72 resulted in agreements that were 'unbalanced' in so far as an *irreversible* West German acceptance of the territorial and political status quo in Central Europe was traded against, firstly, Soviet undertakings (which can be repealed, though at a substantial cost) and sec-ondly, *prospects* for improved relations with the Eastern states, which may not materialise. It is undoubtedly true, as asserted repeatedly by spokesmen of the Brandt government, that nothing was conceded in the agreements that had not been lost as a result of World War II, and that West Germany's formal acceptance of present conditions in Central Europe was a *sine qua non* for Soviet concessions and the opening up of new vistas in relations with the East. Yet, the very nature of this deal is liable to generate continued domestic pressure on the government in Bonn to secure its part of the *quid pro quo*, particularly in terms of further inter-German normalisation. The Federal Republic, more than any of the other parties to the deal, has a vested interest in viewing it in dynamic terms: as the beginning of a process of qualitative change in East-West relations in Europe.

In the case of the Federal Republic, the full exploitation of opportunities for continued *détente* and some measure of *rapprochement* with the East has always presupposed balancing developments conducive to closer collabora-tion in the West. What counts in this respect, however, is not primarily the demonstration of West Germany's loyal adherence to the Western camp, but rather concrete progress in West European integration, which depends on the actions and attitudes of many states. For it is the *reality* rather than the demonstration of West Germany's involvement in dynamically develop-

94

ing Western co-operative schemes and institutions that is likely to determine Bonn's perceptions of the scope for further collaboration with Eastern Europe.

While it can be assumed that the above considerations will be of equal relevance for the calculations of any future West German government, irrespective of its political shading, there are some differences in the specific compulsions and constraints sensed by each of the two major parties in the pursuit of *Ostpolitik*. Undoubtedly the main problem of the CDU/CSU in this regard is to win and sustain sufficient confidence in the East. In the course of recent years leading politicians of the union parties, it is true, have been able to demonstrate with some success their acceptability as serious talking partners in several of the main Eastern capitals. But not only did East Berlin constitute a conspicuous exception to this rule: there is every reason to believe that in the Soviet Union and Poland as well the reservations against the political forces represented by these leaders have remained formidable. Thus, they would seem to be confronted with the task of ensuring that their acceptance of the East-West deal as a working basis for future policy is made credible and that some continuous contact and communication is established with the East German leaders, aiming at the growth of at least a minimum of mutual trust.

The SPD/FDP government has embarked upon a policy of gradual *rapprochement* between the two German states in full awareness of the risks of destabilising repercussions on *both* sides, but particularly in East Germany, as dramatically evinced by the spontaneous demonstrations for Willy Brandt during the first German summit meeting in Erfurt in March 1970. The SPD/FDP leaders have been reasonably confident in their own ability to manage this delicate process without eroding the power basis of governing groups in either of the two German states. The result of the 1972 elections in the FRG clearly vindicated these calculations with regard to West Germany. As far as East Germany is concerned, the policy of the SPD/FDP implies nothing less than a willingness to acquiesce in the consolidation of the existing political system in the GDR, as a necessary precondition of freer communication between the two German states. Since a West German government led by the SPD is particularly vulnerable to the charge of consolidating a communist regime in Germany, it must refrain from proclaiming this goal openly and yet be able to convey a reassuring message to the East German leaders. For the same reason the SPD leadership is forced to draw a sharp line against the recently legalised West German Communist Party and other leftist groups that lack reliable democratic credentials. As the SPD leaders pursue efforts to sustain and widen the opening between the two German states, they must ensure that there is no fuzziness about the distinction between Social Democracy and Communism in the FRG, lest their whole policy be easily discredited as a dangerous operation exposing West Germany to the risk of communist subversion.[2]

The viability of the East German political system was originally based on the assumption of a hostile relationship with Bonn, a challenging attitude toward the political and social institutions in the FRG, and a relentless battle against the ties between West Germany and Berlin, the outpost of the West in the midst of the GDR. The essential reasons for this stand should be sought in the differences characterising the power relations between the two German states with regard to both their material resources and the amount of popular support which their respective governments have been able to mobilise. While the FRG and the GDR belong to different social systems and military alliances, the bonds of common nationhood, however much they have lately been denounced by the East German leaders, constitute a framework within which both German governments are operating. In this context the East German side has seen itself as by far the weaker of the two. Hence the SED's efforts to ensure its power position by *Abgrenzung* towards the West and by strict party control of all aspects of social and political life in East Germany.

The East-West agreements of 1970–72 largely thwarted the East German attempts to invalidate this common framework of inter-German politics. The trend towards alienation between the two German states was halted, if not reversed, and the East German leaders were induced to countenance a limited opening towards the West. This situation generated a natural urge on the part of the SED to re-emphasise its close ties with Moscow.

The set of circumstances, which more than any other considerations, is likely to determine the views of the SED regarding future East-West relations, is the pace and extent of a continued Soviet-West German *rapprochement* on the one hand and the possibilities of consolidating its own domestic power on the other. Only if there is progress in the latter realm – as a result of international recognition abroad and successful economic performance at home – and if the future development of Soviet-West German relations provides a continued incentive for the East German leaders to be 'co-operative', will a controlled opening towards the West appear to the SED both feasible and necessary.

2   From accommodation to co–operation

At the end of 1972 Europe was on the threshold of a new stage in East-West negotiations, which, it could be assumed with some confidence, would be characterised by a growth of multilateralism within the framework of the proposed CSCE, or other negotiating schemes and institutions.[3] A good deal of intellectual and diplomatic effort has been invested in the preparation of these multilateral negotiations.[4] While this is all to the good, since the organisational tasks before the participants in the negotiations are indeed formidable, it should at the same time be recognised that ingenuity in devising blueprints for negotiating frameworks and new institutions is no substitute for the elaboration of effective *policies* conducive to a transition from accommodation to co-operation. The latter presupposes not only a basic commitment to the search for common interests, but also mutual appreciation of the vital preoccupations, as well as the remaining fears and suspicions, of the main actors on the European scene. The preceding analysis was aimed at identifying some of these crucial factors. On the basis of our findings it should now be possible to formulate certain requirements that will have to be met in order to reach a stage in intra-European politics, the distinguishing mark of which would be the evolution of East-West co-operation. We shall again pay special attention to the concerns of the two German states as the most exposed partners on each side.

Assuming that the overriding interest of the two super-powers in keeping their rivalry within bounds will induce them to adopt military and political postures conducive to a low level of East-West tension in Europe, the future of East-West relations is likely to depend on how the wider pan-European processes interact with developments in the two alliances and the West European community. The most fundamental policy requirement that will have to be met, in order to enable the nations of Western and Eastern Europe to engage in mutually advantageous collaboration, is usually referred to by the terms 'stability' and 'balance'. While these concepts are seldom clearly defined they would seem to reflect preoccupation with

1) the possibility of predicting and exerting effective influence on the impact and outcome of evolving processes of change in East-West relations, and

2) the need to ensure that no disadvantages, but, rather, equal advantages accrue to those involved in these processes. These principles also seem to imply a preference for the preservation of existing political and economic structures, or at least for gradual, rather than swift and radical, transformation.[5]

In view of the complexity and rapid change characterising societal and political developments in Europe, the best that can be hoped is that some progress towards 'stability' and 'balance' can be made. Even an approximate satisfaction of these requirements, however, presupposes a better understanding of the nature of co-operation in a pan-European framework marked by distinct asymmetries.

Co-operation enhances contact and mutual interdependence. It therefore gives those involved increased opportunities for exerting influence on each other. However, in the present European context these opportunities are determined by a number of highly asymmetrical conditions. The following are of special importance for the subsequent argument:[6]

97

Western Europe [7]	Eastern Europe
1. Pluralistic social and political systems; relatively sound domestic legitimacy of governing groups.	1. Ideological and social uniformity; lack of domestic legitimacy of ruling elites.
2. Decentralisation of political power, less on the national than on the alliance level.	2. Centralised political control exercised by party elites in individual countries and ultimately by the leadership of the CPSU.
3. Superiority in terms of economic performance as well as scientific and technological know-how.	3. Demand for investment capital and advanced technology.
4. Sub-regional integration process without super-power participation, but with significant involvement of American based multinational corporations.	4. Geographic proximity of super-power, and effective control of sub-regional co-operation by that super-power.

Given these asymmetries, what are the sensitive points one must recognise, if one's concern is to promote the evolution of East-West co-operation for both the benefit of Europe as a whole and the good of the outside world, and not the reaping of more narrowly defined advantages under the guise of 'pan-European co-operation'? Generally speaking they would seem to be the following three:

1) The Soviet Union – as a super-power with a solid territorial basis in Europe, exerting rather effective control over its own allies and being faced with a politically and geographically much more diffuse group of nations – enjoys a potential leeway for manipulating intra-Western differences, particularly semi-latent rivalries between Paris and Bonn on the one hand and between Western Europe (or the European Community) and the United States on the other. This factor is of special importance in a period of extended East-West co-operation, since the pluralistic nature of Western societies makes them susceptible to influence on a variety of levels, the interaction of which the Soviet Union has been able to exploit.[8]

2) On the other hand the Western societies, because of their pluralistic nature, possess a wide variety of means with which they can exert influence. In an era of intensified East-West contact, the use of these means, unless they are handled with great care, tends, in combination with the economic vigour and technological superiority of the West, to erode the power basis of East European ruling elites, and could thus at a certain point jeopardise the overall balance of the process of East-West *rapprochement*. This is specially true of potential developments in inter-German relations.

3) As long as the Soviet Union bases its supremacy in Eastern Europe on

the claim that the CPSU is the only authentic arbiter of the collective interests of the socialist states, the extension of multilateral co-operation between East and West, which is liable to widen the scope for independent action of individual East European states, will be perceived by Moscow as a potential or immediate threat to its vital interests. At some stage in the future, therefore, the Soviet leadership might consider the 'balance' disturbed in the sense that it would deem it impossible to control the impact and outcome of the evolving processes of change in East-West relations.

If these points are valid, a number of conclusions can be derived from them in terms of policy measures, general modes of behaviour and desirable developments that would be conductive to a 'balanced' evolution of East-West co-operation in Europe.

The assured prospect of close political ties between Western Europe and the United States appears a fundamental precondition for 'stability and balance' in future East-West relations. In spite of recent demonstrations of the limited political utility of military power in the nuclear age, political leaders in Western Europe will probably continue to feel uncomfortable about the shift in favour of the East that would result from serious uncertainty about America's commitment to the defence of Western Europe. In view of the symbolic importance of the 'traditional' level of six US divisions in the FRG[9] and the domestic American pressures for troop withdrawals from Europe – mutual and balanced if possible, but unilateral if necessary – there seems to be a need for a conclusive manifestation of America's continued involvement in European security issues over and above the deployment of any given number of US divisions on the Old Continent. In this context the contractual basis for sn American presence in Berlin established by the Four Power Agreement is undoubtedly an asset.[10] Another could emerge from the participation of the United States in such permanent pan-European institutions dealing with security questions as might conceivably be created as a result of a CSCE.[11]

However close political co-operation between Western Europe and the United States is also necessary in order to eliminate effectively the Soviet potential for disrupting the Western alliance by skilful diplomacy on different levels of East-West negotiations or by other, more subtle, methods of exerting influence on individual Western countries. Whether this potential is real or imagined, it is liable to disturb the balance between East and West in a period of intensified co-operation across ideological barriers. But the need for effective demonstration of long-term solidarity among the Western nations will be met only if the present trend towards transatlantic alienation is reversed.

This trend is at present being fed by powerful forces and constitutes a major drawback to all attempts at forging a credible common Western policy towards the East. While it manifests itself primarily in a tug-of-war over monetary and trade issues, its roots are political as much as economic. Since most political questions have an economic aspect, it was unavoidable that the legitimate American concern with burden-sharing within the alliance should become especially acute in the aftermath of the costly Vietnam débacle. For the same reason, the United States Congress was inclined to couple its insistence on adequate West European contributions to the common defence with the question of American force levels in Western Europe and with trade and currency issues. As the public perception of the Soviet threat was at the same time waning, the net effects of these developments was an erosion of the sense of common purpose on both sides of the Atlantic. This situation can be changed only if the intra-Western conflicts in the realm of trade, finance and monetary questions are handled in a frame of mind that will again inspire the peoples of the Western world with a feeling that the common nature of their objectives overrides narrowly defined regional or national interests.[12] Such a reassertion of common Western values and purposes presupposes that America will recover from the most acute phase of its present social and political malaise and that a responsible leadership in Washington will be able to infuse a new sense of direction and self-confidence into its own people. This is not to deny the usefulness of palliatives, such as giving 'an organic form to the dialogue between the United States and the Common Market'[13], but it is equally important to recognise such measures for what they are.

Since a rapid Soviet-West German *rapprochement* could set off a process of dynamic interaction with high stakes on both sides, the relations between these two countries are likely to be viewed by most actors on the European scene as a potential threat to the stability of East-West relations. While there are no signs that Soviet policy makers entertain any hope of weaning away the FRG from its association with the West,[14] Moscow has kept open all options leading in that direction. Consequently, the Soviet Union could help along developments which, resulting, for example, from intensified economic relations between Moscow and Bonn and concomitant West German frustration in the West, might bring about a situation in which West German national interests would reassert themselves at the expense of the FRG's Western orientation. Such a trend, however, would clearly be detrimental to the overall stability of East-West relations in Europe. Significant apprehensions could be expected to arise in the United States, Western Europe and Eastern Europe regarding both the political repercussions of Soviet-West German collaboration and the prospects for ensuring equal advantages to other participants in East-West co-operation in Europe.

A tightening of bilateral bonds between the United States and West Germany would hardly be the right remedy for this contingency, since it would tend to re-emphasise old cold-war structures, which in turn could only hamper the desired East-West developments. Only active West German participation in the progress of West European political and economic integration could eliminate threats to the stability of East-West co-operation in Europe emanating from an accelerating Soviet West-German *rapprochement*.[15] Soviet attitudes towards the European Community should therefore be a test of Moscow's willingness to promote East-West co-operation at the expense of its potential for exploiting some of the asymmetries characterising the situation in Europe.

Given the present outlook of the Soviet leaders and the realities of power in Eastern Europe, deference to Moscow's preferences is liable to impose distinct limits on the efforts of its East European allies at extending the scope and intensity of co-operation with Western Europe. The Soviet Union is likely to exert itself to control East-West trade and financial arrangements through CMEA in order to derive maximum benefit from a growth in the flow of scarce goods and capital and also for the purpose of containing the political repercussions of this process. At the same time it should be recognised that CMEA provides the East European states with an essential instrument of sub-regional co-ordination and co-operation, which they need to ensure some 'balance' in their dealings with the superior economic power of the West.

Western policy postures can only marginally influence developments within CMEA without arousing new suspicions and thus jeopardising the overall development of East-West co-operation. Yet, while containing this risk as far as possible, the West should counteract Soviet efforts to use CMEA as an instrument for asserting its supremacy in Eastern Europe. It should not be beyond the ingenuity of Western politicians to combine such policies with a position clearly demonstrating respect for the legitimate role of the organisation in co-ordinating economic policies of member states and promoting the general development of their economies.

The CSCE could serve a useful purpose in this connection. It could help to establish new patterns of contact and co-operation between individual East and West European states, a development which would tend to de-emphasise the predominance of the Soviet Union in Eastern Europe. On the other hand, the very fact that this would occur within a framework of East-West negotiations, in which both super-powers were represented, could make the emergence of these new patterns of intra-European co-operation – under a kind of US-Soviet 'supervision' – more acceptable to the leading powers in East and West.

Conceivably, the CSCE could also agree on some general principles of co-operation along the lines of those adopted bilaterally by the Soviet Union and France on 30 October 1971.[16] These principles, it is true, do not reflect nearly enough the present trend toward mutual interpenetration of co-operating advanced societies to make them an appropriate 'model' for the future; for, as Marshall Shulman has rightly observed, in the international system of today and tomorrow 'change itself must be the fundamental starting point for any effort to codify relations among nations.'[17] Yet, attempts to establish principles that would correspond to this timely demand are liable to overtax the adaptability and imaginativeness of the present political leaders of most countries in both East *and* West, if not of their advisers as well. In the circumstances the best thing to strive for would seem to be the enunciation of principles of conduct which, while clearly inadequate as a general standard for international relations, would still serve to increase at least marginally the scope for individual nations in Eastern Europe to assert their own interests without jeopardising those of others.

It is probably unrealistic to expect from the CSCE a formal abrogation of the so-called 'Brezhnev doctrine' of state sovereignty being subordinated to the interests of the entire socialist community (as defined by the CPSU leadership). But at least a declaration on the multilateral renunciation of force to be adopted by the CSCE should be formulated in such a way as to exclude the interpretation that it legitimises the use of force *within* alliances or groups of nations belonging to the *same* social system.

Ultimately, the emergence of a pan-European order within which the states of Eastern Europe would be free to follow their own, rather than Moscow's, preferences presupposes that the Soviet Union perceives its own interests in less rigid terms than those reflected in the present preoccupation with ideological uniformity, and in the inclination to ensure it by international party discipline and the stationing of Soviet troops in Eastern Europe.[18] There is no panacea at the disposal of the West to bring about such a change of mind among Soviet leaders, since it could only be the result of fundamental social developments within the Soviet Union and other socialist states. But ironically the very processes that are today a major source of concern to Moscow in the realm of East-West relations, may one day produce a situation in which these apprehensions will appear unwarranted. An incremental, undramatic expansion of cultural contacts and economic interdependence between Eastern and Western Europe may one day conceivably reach a point where neither side has reason to fear an overthrow of its social and political order as a result of further mutual interpenetration.[19] It should be clear that what is envisaged here is *not* the convergence of the two social systems confronting each other in the heart of Europe, but rather a change of perceptions among governing groups conducive to a redefinition of security in terms less burdened with outdated political, military and ideological concepts.[20]

For reasons that have been hinted at in our preceding analysis[21], the kind of development outlined above would meet its greatest difficulties in the relations between the two German states. To the extent that the SED has been willing to countenance an expansion of co-operation with West Germany, it has shown an inclination to concentrate on projects where human contact can be held at a minimum. This attitude, which is not likely to change quickly, should nevertheless allow a substantial growth and intensification of practical co-operation and exchange in a variety of fields as outlined in the Basic Treaty. Beyond this there could also emerge opportunities for tacit understandings (and eventually even for explicit agreements) on common criteria for measuring the effectiveness of societal performance in the two German states. Until recently the climate of confrontation and the overall inferiority of the social system of the GDR as compared with that of the FRG[22] were apt to prevent such ventures in 'competitive co-operation'; West German proposals in that direction were therefore usually interpreted in East Berlin as challenges to the stability of the regime.

However, that situation is changing. Not only has the self-confidence of both leaders and people in the GDR been enhanced by recent events; in a number of fields the East German society has achieved results that can well compare with and in some instances surpass those of the FRG.[23] This development may well continue, and the showing of the GDR may be increasingly impressive, especially if societal performance is measured not in terms of *per capita* income but by the more subtle and timely yardstick of 'the quality of life'. Thus, 'competitive co-operation' between the GDR and the FRG could gain momentum for the benefit of people in the whole of Germany.[24] Yet, it is essential to remember that progress in that direction depends on the preservation and multiplication of the still rather limited capital of mutual trust between Bonn and East Berlin, accumulated during the 1970–72 negotiations. It also presupposes that the agreed *modus vivendi* in Berlin can be transformed into a working relationship, a change which will pose major problems of adaptation to the parties concerned. Since inter-German relations are likely to be a pace-setter of East-West *rapprochement* in Europe, the successful management of remaining difficulties in these relations is not only a German, but also a European, interest.

Notes

[1] Cf Martin Kriele, 'Können die Berliner sicherer leben? Zehn Thesen zum Rahmenabkommen der Vier Mächte' *Die Zeit*, 18 February 1972.
[2] This argument was actually used by the CDU/CSU leaders when pleading against the *Ostpolitik* of the Brandt government. See, for example, Gerhard Schröder, 'Nein zu den Ostverträgen' *Die Zeit*, 4 February 1972.
[3] The formal normalisation of Bonn's relations with Prague and the estab-

lishment of diplomatic relations with Hungary and Bulgaria can be viewed as the unfinished business of the first stage in the era of East-West negotiations in Europe marked by bilateralism.

[4] See, for example, Michael Palmer *The Prospects for a European Security Conference*, European Series no. 18, Chatham House: PEP, London 1971; Gerda Zellentin, *Europa 1985. Gesellschaftliche und politische Entwicklungen in Gesamteuropa*, Bonn 1972, pp. 149 ff; also, Working Group on European Co-operation and Security, 'Some Institutional Suggestions for a System of Security and Co-operation in Europe' *Bulletin of Peace Proposals* 1972:1.

[5] This is implied in numerous official and semi-official pronouncements emanating from both East and West. See, for example, A. Vetrov, 'Economic ties between socialist and capitalist states' *International Affairs* (USSR) 9/1970, p. 11; also declaration of the government of the FRG, 28 October 1969, *Texte* vol 1, p. 35.

[6] For a stimulating discussion of European asymmetries from a slightly different vantage point see Stanley Hoffmann, 'Thoughts on European Security' *Proceedings of the Twenty-first Pugwash Conference on Science and World Affairs*, Sinaia, Romania, 26–31 August 1971, pp. 230 f.

[7] The characteristics enumerated here obviously do not apply to conditions in Spain, Portugal and Greece. This fact, however, is of marginal importance for the overall picture of asymmetries in a pan-European framework.

[8] Cf Zbigniew Brzezinski *Ideology and Power in Soviet Politics*, New York 1962, p. 105.

[9] Cf Hans J. Morgenthau, 'History's Prisoners: Six U.S. Divisions' *International Herald Tribune*, 4 March, 1970.

[10] Cf above p. 93.

[11] This also provides an argument in favour of close institutional links between CSCE and negotiations on MBFR. Cf Christoph Bertram, 'Mutual Force Reductions in Europe' *Adelphi Papers* no. 84, London 1972, p. 31.

[12] For an eloquent argument along the same lines see Richard Löwenthal, 'A World Adrift' *Encounter*, February 1972, pp. 28–29.

[13] Willy Brandt proposed 'an organised dialogue' between the United States and the EEC 'on a high level and with a certain regularity ...'. See his article 'Germany's "Westpolitik"' *Foreign Affairs*, April 1972, p. 421.

[14] Cf. B. D. Melnikov, 'FRG facing crucial choice' *Mirovaya Ekonomika i Mezhdunarodnye Otnoshenia* no. 5/1972.

[15] It goes without saying that appropriate Community policies *vis-à-vis* the East are also required lest East-West co-operation be jeopardised.

[16] See 'Principles of Co-operation between the USSR and France' adopted in connection with Leonid Brezhnev's visit to France 25–30 October 1971, *Soviet News* no. 5612, 2 November 1971, p. 351.

[17] Marshal D. Shulman, 'What does security mean today?' *Foreign Affairs*, July 1971, p. 614.

[18] Cf. Marshall D. Shulman, *op. cit.*, p. 615; also Richard Löwenthal's comment on Nicolaus Sombart, 'Gesamteuropäische Ordnung', in *Aussenpolitische Perspektiven des westdeutschen Staates*, Bd. 1: *Das Ende des Provisoriums*, München-Wien 1971, p. 87.

[19] Cf Gerda Zellentin *Europa 1985*, p. 156.

[20] Marshall D. Shulman has made a commendable first effort to promote thinking in this direction, specifically emphasising 'that spheres of influence, even if granted, cannot under modern conditions provide the basis for stable and productive relations' (Shulman, *op. cit.*, p. 615).

[21] See above, Chapter 3.

[22] See 'Bundesministerium für innerdeutsche Beziehungen' *Bericht der Bundesregierung und Materialien zur Lage der Nation 1971*, pp. 89 ff,

[23] In educational and vocational training, for example, the GDR has a clear lead over the FRG. Cf *ibid.*, pp. 187 ff.

[24] This is in line with concluding remarks made by State Secretary Paul Frank in a speech before the *Deutsche Gesellschaft für Osteuropakunde* on 13 October 1971, *Bulletin* no. 148, 14 October 1971.

Select Bibliography

Arbatov, G. A., 'A step serving the interests of peace' *USA* (Soviet journal), November 1971.

Aussenpolitische Perspektiven des westdeutschen Staates, Bd 1: *Das Ende des Provisoriums*, R. Oldenbourg, München-Wien 1971.

Baylis, Thomas A., 'In quest of legitimacy' *Problems of Communism*, March–April 1972.

Beglov, Spartak I., 'Die aussenpolitische Plattform des XXIV. Parteitages der KPdSU' *Deutsche Aussenpolitik* 5/1971.

Bender, Peter *Die Ostpolitik Willy Brandts oder Die Kunst des Selbstverständlichen*, Rowohlt, Reinbeck bei Hamburg 1972; *6 × Sicherheit: Befürchtungen in Osteuropa*, Kiepenheuer and Witsch, Köln and Berlin 1970.

Bertram, Christoph, 'Mutual force reductions in Europe' *Adelphi Papers* no. 84, London 1972.

Birnbaum, Karl E. *Peace in Europe: East-West relations 1966–1968 and the prospects for a European settlement*, Oxford University Press, London, Oxford and New York 1970.

Birrenbach, Kurt *Aussenpolitik nach der Wahl des 6. Bundestages (Aktuelle Aussenpolitik)*, C. W. Leske Verlag, Opladen 1969.

Brandt, Willy, 'Germany's "Westpolitik"' *Foreign Affairs*, April 1972.

Brzezinski, Z *Ideology and power in Soviet politics*, Frederick A. Praeger, New York 1962.

Chossudovsky, Evgeny, 'Genoa revisited: Russia and coexistence' *Foreign Affairs*, April 1972.

Croan, Melvin, 'After Ulbricht: the end of an era?' *Survey* no. 17 (February 1971); 'Czechoslovakia, Ulbricht and the German Problem' *Problems of Communism* 18/1, January 1969.

Domdey K. H., 'The efforts of the GDR to establish normal economic relations with capitalist states: a case of peaceful coexistence' *Co-existence* 9/1, January 1972.

Feist, Manfred, 'Die Autorität der DDR wächts trotz imperialistischer Manöver' *Einheit* 9/1971.

Franke, Paul, 'Sicherheitsprobleme im Lichte des Moskauer Vertrags' *Europa-Archiv* 24/1970.

Gorokhov A, 'The USSR's struggle for European security' *International Affairs (USSR)* 1/1971.

Hoffmann, Stanley, 'Thoughts on European security' *Proceedings of the Twenty-first Pugwash Conference on Science and World Affairs*, Sinaia, Romania, 26–31 August 1971.

Hänisch W. and Krüger J. 'Zur Dialektik von Innen- und Aussenpolitik in der Strategie und Taktik der SED' *Deutsche Aussenpolitik* 3/1971.

Johnson, A. Ross, 'The Warsaw Pact's campaign for European security' *Rand Report*, R-565-PR, November 1970.

Korbel, Josef *Détente in Europe: Real or Imaginary?* Princeton University Press, Princeton 1972.

Ludz, Peter, 'Continuity and change since Ulbricht' *Problems of Communism*, March-April 1972; *The German Democratic Republic from the Sixties to the Seventies. A Socio-Political Analysis*, Occasional Papers in International Affairs no. 26 (November 1970) Harvard University, Center for International Affairs; 'Zum Begriff der "Nation" in der Sicht der SED. Wandlungen und politische Bedeutung' *Deutschland-Archiv* 1/1972.

Löwenthal, Richard, 'Kreml am Kreuzweg. Stalin's Schatten liegt über der Ostpolitik' *Die Zeit*, 19 February 1971; 'A world adrift' *Encounter* 2/1972.

Oppermann, Thomas, 'Deutsche Einheit und europäische Friedensordnung: Perspektiven nach dem Moskauer Vertrag' *Europa-Archiv* 3/1971.

Palmer, Michael, *The prospects for a European security conference*, European Series no. 18, Chatham House: PEP, London 1971.

Popov, K., 'West European integration and international cooperation' *Voprosy Ekonomiki* 1/1971.

Shulman, Marshall D. 'What does security mean?' *Foreign Affairs*, July 1971.

Spittmann, Ilse, 'Warum Ulbricht stürtze' *Deutschland Archiv* 6/1971.

Ulam, Adam B. *Expansion and Coexistence: the History of Soviet Foreign Policy 1917–1967*, Frederick A. Praeger, New York and London 1968.

Vetrov, A., Economic ties between socialist and capitalist states' *International Affairs* 9/1970.

Wagner, Wolfgang, 'Towards a new political order: German Ostpolitik and the East-West realignment' *International Journal* 27/1, Winter 1971–72.

Wettig, Gerhard, *Europäische Sicherheit. Das europäische Staatensystem in der sowjetischen Aussenpolitik 1966–1972*, Bertelsmann Universitätsverlag (Veröffentlichungen des Bundesinstituts für osteuropäische und internationale Studien) Köln 1972.

Wolfe, Thomas W. *Soviet Power and Europe 1945–1970*, The John Hopkins Press, Baltimore and London 1970.

Zellentin, Gerda *Europa 1985. Gesellschaftliche und politische Entwicklungen in Gesamteuropa*, Europa Union Verlag GmbH, Bonn 1972; *Intersystemare Beziehungen in Europa. Bedingungen der Friedenssicherung*, A. W. Sijthoff, Leiden 1970.

Basic Documents

'Appeal issued by the Political Consultative Committee of the Warsaw Treaty Member States at their meeting in Budapest, 17 March 1969' *Soviet News* no. 5841, 18 March 1969.

Bericht der Bundesregierung und Materialien zur Lage der Nation 1971. Bundesministerium für innerdeutsche Beziehungen. [Kassel 1971].

'Declaration on Peace, Security and Co-operation in Europe' adopted by the Political Consultative Committee of the Warsaw Treaty Member States at their meeting in Prague 25–26 January 1972': *Pravda*, 27 January 1972; *Soviet News* no. 5624, 1 February 1972.

Erfurt, March 19, 1970. A Documentation, Press and Information Office of the Government of the Federal Republic of Germany, Bonn [1970].

Government Declaration by Mr. Willy Brandt as Federal Chancellor on 28 October 1969. *Protokoll der 5. Sitzung des Deutschen Bundestages vom 28. Okt. 1969.* English translation *Survival*, December 1969.

Inter-German Agreements implementing the Quadripartite Agreement on Berlin. *Bulletin* no. 183, 11 December 1971.

Kassel, May 21, 1970. A Documentation, Press and Information Office of the Government of the Federal Republic of Germany, Opladen [1970].

The Quadripartite Agreement on Berlin, Sept. 3, 1971, Press and Information Office of the Government of the Federal Republic of Germany, Wiesbaden [1971].

'Principles of co-operation between the USSR and France', issued 30 October 1971 on the occasion of Soviet Party Leader Leonid Brezhnev's visit to France, *Soviet News* no. 5612, 2 November 1972.

Speech by Press Secretary Mr. Egon Bahr on 15 July 1963, before the Evangelische Akademie, Tutzing, on Relations with East Germany. Siegler, H. (ed.) *Wiedervereinigung und Sicherheit Deutschlands* vol. 1, 5th ed. Bonn-Zürich-Wien 1964, pp. 311 ff.

Speech by Soviet Party Leader Leonid Brezhnev before the 15th Congress of Soviet Trade Unions on 20 March 1972: *Pravda*, 21 March 1972; *Soviet News* no. 5632, 28 March 1972.

The Treaty between the Federal Republic of Germany and the People's Republic of Poland, Press and Information Office of the Federal Republic of Germany, Wiesbaden [1971].

Treaty between the German Democratic Republic and the Federal Republic of Germany on Questions Relating to Traffic, unofficial translation, [East] Berlin, May 1972.

Vertrag über die Grundlagen der Beziehungen zwischen der Bundesrepublic Deutschland und der Deutschen Demokratischen Republik, Presse- und Informationsamt der Bundesregierung, [Bonn 1972].

Der Vertrag vom 12. August 1970 zwischen der Bundesrepublik und der Union der Sozialistischen Sowjetrepubliken, Presse- und Informationsamt der Bundesregierung [Bonn 1970].

VIII. Parteitag der SED, Berlin 15.–19. Juni 1971. Bericht des Zentralkomitees Berichterstatter: Genosse Erich Honecker, Berlin 1971.

24th Congress of the CPSU, March 30–April 9. Documents, Novosti Press Agency Publishing House, Moscow 1971.

Appendix 1

Treaty between the Federal Republic of Germany and the Union of Soviet Socialist Republics

The High Contracting Parties

Anxious to contribute to strengthening peace and security in Europe and the world,

Convinced that peaceful co-operation among States on the basis of the purposes and principles of the Charter of the United Nations complies with the ardent desire of nations and the general interests of international peace,

Appreciating the fact that the agreed measures previously implemented by them, in particular the conclusion of the Agreement of 13 September 1955 on the Establishment of Diplomatic Relations, have created favourable conditions for new important steps destined to develop further and to strengthen their mutual relations,

Desiring to lend expression, in the form of a treaty, to their determination to improve and extend co-operation between them, including economic relations as well as scientific, technological and cultural contacts, in the interest of both States,

Have agreed as follows:

Article 1

The Federal Republic of Germany and the Union of Soviet Socialist Republics consider it an important objective of their policies to maintain international peace and achieve détente.

They affirm their endeavour to further the normalization of the situation in Europe and the development of peaceful relations among all European States, and in so doing proceed from the actual situation existing in this region.

Article 2

The Federal Republic of Germany and the Union of Soviet Socialist Republics shall in their mutual relations as well as in matters of ensuring European and international security be guided by the purposes and principles embodied in the Charter of the United Nations. Accordingly they shall settle their disputes exclusively by peaceful means and undertake to refrain from the threat or use of force, pursuant to Article 2 of the Charter of the United Nations, in any matters affecting security in Europe or international security as well as in their mutual relations.

Article 3

In accordance with the foregoing purposes and principles the Federal Republic of Germany and the Union of Soviet Socialist Republics share the realization that peace can only be maintained in Europe if nobody disturbs the present frontiers.

- They undertake to respect without restriction the territorial integrity of all States in Europe within their present frontiers;
- they declare that they have no territorial claims against anybody nor will assert such claims in the future;
- they regard today and shall in future regard the frontiers of all States in Europe as inviolable such as they are on the date of signature of the present Treaty, including the Oder-Neisse line which forms the western frontier of the People's Republic of Poland and the frontier between the Federal Republic of Germany and the German Democratic Republic.

Article 4

The present Treaty between the Federal Republic of Germany and the Union of Soviet Socialist Republics shall not affect any bilateral or multilateral treaties or arrangements previously concluded by them.

Article 5

The present Treaty is subject to ratification and shall enter into force on the date of exchange of the instruments of ratification which shall take place in Bonn.

Done at Moscow on 12 August 1970 in two originals, each in the German and Russian languages, both texts being equally authentic.

<table>
<tr><td>For the
Federal Republic
of Germany
Willy Brandt
Walter Scheel</td><td>For the
Union of Soviet
Socialist Republics
Alexei N. Kosygin
Andrei A. Gromyko</td></tr>
</table>

Letter on German Unity

On the occasion of the signing of the Treaty, the Federal Government handed over in the Soviet Foreign Ministry the following letter:

Dear Mr. Minister

In connection with today's signature of the Treaty between the Federal Republic of Germany and the Union of Soviet Socialist Republics the

Government of the Federal Republic of Germany has the honour to state that this Treaty does not conflict with the political objective of the Federal Republic of Germany to work for a state of peace in Europe in which the German nation will recover its unity in free self-determination.

I assure you, Mr. Minister, of my highest esteem.

Walter Scheel

Text of Notes sent to the Embassies of France, the United Kingdom and the United States in Moscow

On August 7, 1970, before the initialling of the Treaty between the Federal Republic of Germany and the Union of Soviet Socialist Republics, Verbal Notes to the same effect were handed to the Ambassadors of the Three Western Powers in Moscow.

The following is the text of the Verbal Note of the Embassy of the Federal Republic of Germany to the Embassy of the United States of America:

Embassy
of the
Federal Republic of Germany
in Moscow   August 7, 1970

The Embassy of the Federal Republic of Germany greets the Embassy of the United States of America and has the honour on behalf of its Government to hand over the following Note with the request that its contents be brought to the notice of the Government of the United States by the most rapid channels:

The Government of the Federal Republic of Germany has the honour, in connection with the imminent signing of a Treaty between the Federal Republic of Germany and the Union of Soviet Socialist Republics, to communicate the following:

The Federal Minister for Foreign Affairs has, in the context of the negotiations, set forth the Federal Government's position as regards the rights and responsibilities of the Four Powers with regard to Germany as a whole and Berlin.

Since a peace settlement is still outstanding, both sides proceeded on the understanding that the proposed Treaty does not affect the rights and responsibilities of the French Republic, the United Kingdom of Great Britain and Northern Ireland, the Union of Soviet Socialist Republics and the United States of America.

The Federal Minister for Foreign Affairs has in this connection declared to the Soviet Foreign Minister on 6 August 1970:

"The question of the rights of the Four Powers is in no way connected with the Treaty which the Federal Republic of Germany and the Union of Soviet Socialist Republics intend to conclude, and will not be affected by it."

The Foreign Minister of the Union of Soviet Socialist Republics thereupon made the following declaration:

"The question of the rights of the Four Powers was not the subject of negotiations with the Federal Republic of Germany.

"The Soviet Government proceeded on the understanding that this question should not be discussed.

"Nor will the question of the rights of the Four Powers be affected by the Treaty which the U.S.S.R. and the Federal Republic of Germany intend to conclude. This is the position of the Soviet Government regarding this question."

The Embassy of the Federal Republic of Germany avails itself of this opportunity to renew to the Embassy of the United States the assurance of its high consideration.

Notes to the same effect were sent to the French Embassy in Moscow and to the Embassy of the United Kingdom of Great Britain and Northern Ireland in Moscow.

The Notes of the Western powers

The Governments of the Three Western Powers have likewise passed Notes to the same effect to the Federal Government on August 11, 1970, in Bonn as reply. The following is the text of the Note of the Government of the United States of America:

Embassy
   of the
United States of America
  Bonn-Bad Godesberg   August 11, 1970

The Government of the United States of America has the honour of informing the Government of the Federal Republic of Germany that it has received the following note transmitted by the Government of the Federal Republic of Germany on 7th of August, 1970:

The Government of the Federal Republic of Germany has the honour, in connection with the imminent signing of a Treaty between the Federal

112

Republic of Germany and the Union of Soviet Socialist Republics, to communicate the following:

The Federal Minister of Foreign Affairs has, in the context of the negotiations, set forth the Federal Government's position as regards the rights and responsibilities of the Four Powers with regard to Germany as a whole and Berlin.

Since a peace settlement is still outstanding, both sides proceeded on the understanding that the proposed Treaty does not affect the rights and responsibilities of the French Republic, the United Kingdom of Great Britain and Northern Ireland, the Union of Soviet Socialist Republics and the United States of America.

The Federal Minister for Foreign Affairs has in this connection declared to the Soviet Foreign Minister on 6 August 1970:

"The question of the rights of the Four Powers is in no way connected with the Treaty which the Federal Republic of Germany and the Union of Soviet Socialist Republics intend to conclude, and will not be affected by it."

The Foreign Minister of the Union of Soviet Socialist Republics thereupon made the following declaration:

"The question of the rights of the Four Powers was not the subject of negotiations with the Federal Republic of Germany.

"The Soviet Government proceeded on the understanding that this question should not be discussed.

"Nor will the question of the rights of the Four Powers be affected by the Treaty which the U.S.S.R. and the Federal Republic of Germany intend to conclude. This is the position of the Soviet Government regarding this question."

The Government of the United States takes full cognizance of this Note, including the declarations made by the Foreign Minister of the Federal Republic of Germany and the Foreign Minister of the Union of Soviet Socialist Republics as part of the negotiations prior to the initialling of the treaty which is to be concluded between the Federal Republic of Germany and the Soviet Union.

For its part, the Government of the United States also considers that the rights and responsibilities of the Four Powers for Berlin and Germany as a whole which derive from the outcome of the Second World War and which are reflected in the London Agreement of November 14, 1944, and in the Quadripartite Declaration of June 5, 1945, and in other wartime and postwar agreements, are not and cannot be affected by a bilateral treaty between the Federal Republic of Germany and the Union of Soviet Socialist Republics, including the present treaty.

Bahr Paper

1

The Federal Republic of Germany and the Union of Soviet Socialist Republics consider it an important objective of their policies to maintain international peace and achieve détente.

They affirm their endeavour to further the normalization of the situation in Europe and in doing so to proceed from the actual situation existing in this region and the development of peaceful relations on this basis among all European States.

2

In their mutual relations as well as in matters of ensuring European and international security, the Federal Republic of Germany and the Union of Soviet Socialist Republics shall be guided by the purposes and principles embodied in the statutes of the United Nations.

Accordingly, they will settle their disputes exclusively by peaceful means and undertake to refrain from the threat or use of force in any matters affecting security in Europe or internationally as well as in their mutual relations pursuant to Article 2 of the statutes of the United Nations.

3

The Federal Republic of Germany and the Soviet Union share the realization that peace in Europe can be maintained only if no one disturbs the present frontiers.

They undertake to respect without restriction the territorial integrity of all States in Europe within their present frontiers.

They declare they have no territorial claims against anybody, nor will assert such claims in the future.

They regard today and shall in future regard the frontiers of all States in Europe as inviolable such as they are on the date of signature of this agreement, including the Oder-Neisse Line, which forms the western frontier of the People's Republic of Poland, and the frontier between the Federal Republic of Germany and the German Democratic Republic.

4

The agreement between the Federal Republic of Germany and the Union of Soviet Socialist Republics shall not affect the bilateral or multilateral treaties and agreements previously concluded by the two sides.

5

Agreement exists between the Government of the Federal Republic of

Germany and the Government of the Union of Soviet Socialist Republics that the agreement on ... (the official designation of the agreemten to be inserted) to be concluded by them and corresponding agreements (treaties) of the Federal Republic of Germany with other socialist countries, in particular agreements (treaties) with the German Democratic Republic (see 6), the People's Republic of Poland and the Czechoslovak Socialist Republic (see 8) form a homogeneous whole.

6

The Government of the Federal Republic of Germany declares its preparedness to conclude an agreement with the Government of the German Democratic Republic that shall have the same binding force, usual between States, as other agreements the Federal Republic of Germany and the German Democratic Republic conclude with third countries. Accordingly, it will frame its relations with the German Democratic Republic on the basis of full equality of status, non-discrimination, respect for the independence and autonomy of both States in matters concerning their internal competency within their respective frontiers.

The Government of the Federal Republic of Germany proceeds on the premise that the relations of the German Democratic Republic and the Federal Republic of Germany with third States will develop on this basis, in accordance with which neither of the two States can represent the other abroad or act on its behalf.

7

The Government of the Federal Republic of Germany and the Government of the Union of Soviet Socialist Republics declare their preparedness, in the course of the détente in Europe and in the interest of the improvement of the relations among the European countries, in particular the Federal Republic of Germany and the German Democratic Republic, to take steps resulting from their appropriate status to support the accession of the Federal Republic of Germany and the German Democratic Republic to the Organization of the United Nations and its specialized agencies.

8

Agreement exists between the Government of the Federal Republic of Germany and the Government of the Union of Soviet Socialist Republics that the issues connected with the invalidation of the Munich Agreement are to be settled in negotiations between the Federal Republic of Germany and the Czechoslovak Socialist Republic in a form acceptable to both sides.

9

The Government of the Federal Republic of Germany and the Government of the Union of Soviet Socialist Republics, in the interest of both sides and the strengthening of peace in Europe, will continue to develop the economic, scientific, technological, cultural and other relations between the Federal Republic of Germany and the Union of Soviet Socialist Republics.

10

The Government of the Federal Republic of Germany and the Government of the Union of Soviet Socialist Republics welcome the plan of a conference on matters concerning the strengthening of security and cooperation in Europe and will do everything that depends on them for its preparation and successful prosecution.

Source: The Treaty of August 12, 1970 between the Federal Republic of Germany and the Union of Soviet Socialist Republics, published by the Press & Information Office of the Government of the Federal Republic of Germany. [Wiesbaden, 1970]

Appendix 2

Treaty between the Federal Republic of Germany and the People's Republic of Poland concerning the basis for normalizing their mutual relations

The Federal Republic of Germany
and
The People's Republic of Poland

Considering that more than 25 years have passed since the end of the Second World War of which Poland became the first victim and which inflicted great suffering on the nations of Europe,

Conscious that in both countries a new generation has meanwhile grown up to whom a peaceful future should be secured,

Desiring to establish durable foundations for peaceful coexistence and the development of normal and good relations between them,

Anxious to strengthen peace and security in Europe,

Aware that the inviolability of frontiers and respect for the territorial integrity and sovereignty of all States in Europe within their present frontiers are a basic condition for peace,

Have agreed as follows:

Article I

1) The Federal Republic of Germany and the People's Republic of Poland state in mutual agreement that the existing boundary line the course of which is laid down in Chapter IX of the Decisions of the Potsdam Conference of 2 August 1945 as running from the Baltic Sea immediately west of Swinemunde, and thence along the Oder River to the confluence of the western Neisse River and along the western Neisse to the Czechoslovak frontier, shall constitute the western State frontier of the People's Republic of Poland.

2) They reaffirm the inviolability of their existing frontiers now and in the future and undertake to respect each other's territorial integrity without restriction.

3) They declare that they have no territorial claims whatsoever against each other and that they will not assert such claims in the future.

Article II

1) The Federal Republic of Germany and the People's Republic of Poland shall in their mutual relations as well as in matters of ensuring European and

international security be guided by the purposes and principles embodied in the Charter of the United Nations.

2) Accordingly they shall, pursuant to Articles 1 and 2 of the Charter of the United Nations, settle all their disputes exclusively by peaceful means and refrain from any threat or use of force in matters affecting European and international security and in their mutual relations.

Article III

1) The Federal Republic of Germany and the People's Republic of Poland shall take further steps towards full normalization and a comprehensive development of their mutual relations of which the present Treaty shall form the solid foundation.

2) They agree that a broadening of their co-operation in the sphere of economic, scientific, technological, cultural and other relations is in their mutual interest.

Article IV

The present Treaty shall not affect any bilateral or multilateral international arrangements previously concluded by either Contracting Party or concerning them.

Article V

The present Treaty is subject to ratification and shall enter into force on the date of exchange of the instruments of ratification which shall take place in Bonn.

In witness whereof, the Plenipotentiaries of the Contracting Parties have signed the present Treaty.

Done at Warsaw on December 7, 1970 in two originals, each in the German and Polish languages, both texts being equally authentic.

<table>
<tr><td>For the
Federal Republic
of Germany
Willy Brandt
Walter Scheel</td><td>For the
People's Republic
of Poland
Józef Cyrankiewicz
Stefan Jedrychowski</td></tr>
</table>

Text of notes sent to the three Western powers

The Treaty between the Federal Republic of Germany and the People's Republic of Poland having been initialled on 18 November 1970, identical Notes Verbales were transmitted to the Ambassadors of the Three Western Powers in Bonn on 19 November 1970.

Below is the translated text of the Note Verbale transmitted to the Embassy of the United Kingdom of Great Britain and Northern Ireland:

German Federal
Foreign Office   Bonn, November 19, 1970

The German Federal Foreign Office presents its compliments to Her Britannic Majesty's Embassy and has the honour to communicate to the Embassy the following text of a note of today's date of the Government of the Federal Republic of Germany to the Government of the United Kingdom of Great Britain and Northern Ireland:

The Government of the Federal Republic of Germany has the honour to inform the Government of the United Kingdom of Great Britain and Northern Ireland of the attached text of a Treaty between the Federal Republic of Germany and the People's Republic of Poland concerning the Basis for Normalizing their Mutual Relations, which was initialled on the 18th of November, 1970 in Warsaw.

In the course of the negotiations which took place between the Government of the Federal Republic of Germany and the Government of the People's Republic of Poland concerning this Treaty, it was made clear by the Federal Government that the Treaty between the Federal Republic of Germany and the People's Republic of Poland does not and cannot affect the rights and responsibilities of the French Republic, the United Kingdom of Great Britain and Northern Ireland, the Union of Soviet Socialist Republics, and the United States of America as reflected in the known treaties and agreements. The Federal Government further pointed out that it can act only in the name of the Federal Republic of Germany.

The Government of the French Republic and the Government of the United States of America have received identical notes.

The Federal Foreign Office avails itself of this opportunity to renew to Her Britannic Majesty's Embassy the assurances of its highest consideration.

The Notes of the Western powers

On 19 November 1970 the Governments of the Three Western Powers in Bonn likewise handed over identical notes in reply to the Federal Government. Below is the text of the note transmitted by the Government of the United Kingdom of Great Britain and Northern Ireland:

Her Britannic Majesty's Embassy

Bonn, November 19, 1970

Her Britannic Majesty's Embassy present their compliments to the Federal Ministry for Foreign Affairs and, on the instructions of Her Majesty's Principal Secretary of State for Foreign and Commonwealth Affairs, have the honour to transmit the enclosed Note Verbale:

119

Her Majesty's Government in the United Kingdom have the honour to inform the Government of the Federal Republic of Germany that they have received the Note of the Government of the Federal Republic of Germany of the 19th of November, 1970, enclosing the text of the Treaty between the Federal Republic of Germany and the People's Republic of Poland concerning the Basis for Normalising their Mutual Relations, which was initialled on the 18th of November, 1970 in Warsaw and reading as follows:

"The Government of the Federal Republic of Germany has the honour to inform the Government of the United Kingdom of Great Britain and Northern Ireland of the attached text of a Treaty between the Federal Republic of Germany and the People's Republic of Poland concerning the Basis for Normalizing their Mutual Relations, which was initialled on the 18th of November, 1970 in Warsaw.

"In the course of the negotiations which took place between the Government of the Federal Republic of Germany and the Government of the People's Republic of Poland concerning this Treaty, it was made clear by the Federal Government that the Treaty between the Federal Republic of Germany and the People's Republic of Poland does not and cannot affect the rights and responsibilities of the French Republic, the United Kingdom of Great Britain and Northern Ireland, the Union of Soviet Socialist Republics, and the United States of America as reflected in the known treaties and agreements. The Federal Government further pointed out that it can act only in the name of the Federal Republic of Germany.

The Government of the French Republic and the Government of the United States of America have received identical Notes."

Her Majesty's Government note with approval the initialling of the Treaty. They share the position that the Treaty does not and cannot affect the rights and responsibilities of the Four Powers as reflected in the known treaties and agreements.

Her Britannic Majesty's Embassy avail themselves of this opportunity to renew to the Ministry the assurance of their highest consideration.

Information by the Government of the People's Republic of Poland

The Government of the People's Republic of Poland has communicated to the Federal Government the following information on measures for a solution of humanitarian problems:

1

In 1955 the Polish Government recommended the Polish Red Cross to conclude an agreement with the Red Cross of the Federal Republic of Germany

120

on the reunion of families; under that agreement, roughly one quarter million people left Poland up to 1959. Between 1960 and 1969, an additional 150,000 people have departed from Poland under normal procedures. In carrying out measures to reunite families, the Polish Government has been guided above all by the humanitarian motives. However, it could not, and still cannot, agree that its favourable attitude regarding such reunions be exploited for the emigration of Polish nationals for employment purposes.

2

To this day, there have remained in Poland for various reasons (e.g., close ties with their place of birth) a certain number of persons of indisputable ethnic German origin and persons from mixed families whose predominant feeling over the past years has been that they belong to that ethnic group. The Polish Government still holds the view that any persons who owing to their indisputable ethnic German origin wish to leave for either of the two German States may do so subject to the laws and regulations applicable in Poland.

Furthermore, consideration will be given to the situation of mixed and separated families as well as to such cases of Polish nationals, who either because of their changed family situation or because they have changed their earlier decision, express the wish to be reunited with near relatives in the Federal Republic of Germany or in the German Democratic Republic.

3

The appropriate Polish authorities have not received anything like the number of applications from persons wishing to leave the country for the FRG as is maintained in the FRG. According to the inquiries so far made by the Polish authorities, some tens of thousands of people may fall under the criteria possibly entitling them to leaving Poland for the FRG or the GDR. The Polish Government will therefore issue appropriate instructions for careful examination of whether the applications submitted are justified, and for their early consideration.

The Polish Government will authorize the Polish Red Cross to receive from the Red Cross of the FRG lists of the persons whose applications are held by the German Red Cross in order that they may be compared with the lists held by the appropriate Polish authorities, and carefully examined.

4

Co-operation between the Polish Red Cross and the Red Cross of the FRG will be facilitated in any way necessary. The Polish Red Cross will be authorized to receive from the German Red Cross explanatory comments on the lists, and will inform the German Red Cross of the outcome of examinations by the Polish authorities of transmitted applications. The Polish Red Cross will further be authorized to consider jointly with the Red Cross of the FRG all practical questions that might arise from this action.

5

As regards the traffic of persons in connection with visits to relatives, the appropriate Polish authorities will, after the entry into force of the Treaty concerning the Basis for Normalizing Relations between the two States, apply the same principles as are customary with regard to other States of Western Europe.

Joint communiqué on the visit of the Federal Chancellor to Warsaw

At the invitation of the Chairman of the Council of Ministers of the People's Republic of Poland, Józef Cyrankiewicz, the Chancellor of the Federal Republic of Germany, Willy Brandt, paid an official visit to Warsaw from December 6–8, 1970. He was accompanied by the Federal Chancellor's Deputy and Federal Minister for Foreign Affairs, Walter Scheel, the State-Secretaries Egon Bahr, Conrad Ahlers and Georg Ferdinand Duckwitz, and a number of personalities eminent in the political, cultural and economic spheres.

On December 7, 1970, Federal Chancellor Brandt and Federal Foreign Minister Scheel, together with the Chairman of the Council of Ministers Cyrankiewicz and Foreign Minister Jedrychowski, signed the treaty between the Federal Republic of Germany and the People's Republic of Poland concerning the basis for normalizing their mutual relations.

During the visit a talk took place between the Federal Chancellor and the First Secretary of the Central Committee of the Polish United Workers' Party, Vladislav Gomulka. Federal Chancellor Willy Brandt and Federal Foreign Minister Scheel also had talks with the Chairman of the Council of Ministers, Józef Cyrankiewicz, and Foreign Minister Stefan Jedrychowski.

The personalities accompanying the Federal Chancellor had the opportunity to engage in talks with corresponding representatives on the Polish side.

The talks took place in an objective atmosphere and proved useful and fruitful.

Both sides put forward their points of view with complete clarity. They expressed their satisfaction at the signing of the treaty and stated that its realization should write an end to the past and create the prior conditions for a turning-point in the relations between the two States. They agreed that directly after the treaty comes into force the Federal Republic of Germany and the People's Republic of Poland will establish diplomatic relations with one another.

In the view of both sides, the normalization process inaugurated with the signing of the treaty is to pave the way for the resolution of the problems still existing in the sphere of international and human relations.

Both sides have affirmed their determination, guided by the terms of the treaty signed by them, to take further steps towards the complete normalization and comprehensive development of their relations. This applies particularly in the economic, scientific, technological and cultural spheres.

In the process to the normalization a special role falls to the share of the young people of the two countries.

Both sides are agreed that, as a basis for the normalization of the relations between the Federal Republic of Germany and the People's Republic of Poland, the treaty signed is not only of great importance for both States but also represents a vital contribution towards détente in Europe.

Both sides engaged in a detailed exchange of views on a number of current problems connected with the present international situation. They declare their faith in the principle of the peaceful cooperation of countries for mutual advantage, irrespective of different orders of society. They advocate a further reduction of tensions and will encourage the preparation and successful prosecution of a conference on questions of security and cooperation in Europe.

Both sides regard it as desirable to continue at appropriate levels the exchange of views on questions of joint interest. In particular, they have decided to create institutional forms for the joint discussion of problems connected with the extension of the economic cooperation between the two countries.

The Federal Chancellor of the Federal Republic of Germany, Willy Brandt, invited the Chairman of the Council of Ministers of the People's Republic of Poland, Józef Cyrankiewicz, to pay an official visit to the Federal Republic of Germany. This invitation was accepted; the date of the visit will be fixed later.

Source: The Treaty between the Federal Republic of Germany and the People's Republic of Poland, published by the Press and Information Office of the Government of the Federal Republic of Germany. [Wiesbaden, 1971]

Appendix 3

Quadripartite agreement [on Berlin]

The Governments of the United States of America, the French Republic, the Union of Soviet Socialist Republics and the United Kingdom of Great Britain and Northern Ireland,

Represented by their Ambassadors, who held a series of meetings in the building formerly occupied by the Allied Control Council in the American Sector of Berlin,

Acting on the basis of their quadripartite rights and responsibilities, and of the corresponding wartime and postwar agreements and decisions of the Four Powers, which are not affected,

Taking into account the existing situation in the relevant area,

Guided by the desire to contribute to practical improvements of the situation,

Without prejudice to their legal positions,

Have agreed on the following:

Part I: General provisions

1   The four Governments will strive to promote the elimination of tension and the prevention of complications in the relevant area.

2   The four Governments, taking into account their obligations under the Charter of the United Nations, agree that there shall be no use or threat of force in the area and that disputes shall be settled solely by peaceful means.

3   The four Governments will mutually respect their individual and joint rights and responsibilities, which remain unchanged.

4   The four Governments agree that, irrespective of the differences in legal views, the situation which has developed in the area, and as it is defined in this Agreement as well as in the other agreements referred to in this Agreement, shall not be changed unilaterally.

Part II: Provisions relating to the Western Sectors of Berlin

A   The Government of the Union of Soviet Socialist Republics declares that transit traffic by road, rail and waterways through the territory of the German Democratic Republic of civilian persons and goods between the Western Sectors of Berlin and the Federal Republic of Germany will be unimpeded; that such traffic will be facilitated so as to take place in the most simple and expeditious manner; and that it will receive preferential treatment.

Detailed arrangements concerning this civilian traffic, as set forth in Annex I, will be agreed by the competent German authorities.

B   The Governments of the French Republic, the United Kingdom and the United States of America declare that the ties between the Western Sectors of Berlin and the Federal Republic of Germany will be maintained and developed, taking into account that these Sectors continue not to be a constituent part of the Federal Republic of Germany and not to be governed by it.

Detailed arrangements concerning the relationship between the Western Sectors of Berlin and the Federal Republic of Germany are set forth in Annex II.

C   The Government of the Union of Soviet Socialist Republics declares that communications between the Western Sectors of Berlin and areas bordering on these Sectors and those areas of the German Democratic Republic which do not border on these Sectors will be improved. Permanent residents of the Western Sectors of Berlin will be able to travel to and visit such areas for compassionate, family, religious, cultural or commercial reasons, or as tourists, under conditions comparable to those applying to other persons entering these areas.

The problems of the small enclaves, including Steinstuecken, and of other small areas may be solved by exchange of territory.

Detailed arrangements concerning travel, communications and the exchange of territory, as set forth in Annex III, will be agreed by the competent German authorities.

D   Representation abroad of the interests of the Western Sectors of Berlin and consular activities of the Union of Soviet Socialist Republics in the Western Sectors of Berlin can be exercised as set forth in Annex IV.

Part III: Final provisions

This Quadripartite Agreement will enter into force on the date specified in a Final Quadripartite Protocol to be concluded when the measures envisaged in Part II of this Quadripartite Agreement and in its Annexes have been agreed.

Done at the building formerly occupied by the Allied Control Council in the American Sector of Berlin this 3rd day of September 1971, in four originals, each in the English, French and Russian languages, all texts being equally authentic.

For the Government of the United States of America:

Kenneth Rush

For the Government of the French Republic:

Jean Sauvagnargues

For the Government of the Union of Soviet Socialist Republics:

Pyotr A. Abrasimov

For the Government of the United Kingdom of Great Britain and Northern Ireland:

Roger Jackling

Annex I

Communication From the Government of the Union of Soviet Socialist Republics to the Governments of the French Republic, the United Kingdom and the United States of America

The Government of the Union of Soviet Socialist Republics, with reference to Part II (A) of the Quadripartite Agreement of this date and after consultation and agreement with the Government of the German Democratic Republic, has the honor to inform the Governments of the French Republic, the United Kingdom and the United States of America that:

1   Transit traffic by road, rail and waterways through the territory of the German Democratic Republic of civilian persons and goods between the Western Sectors of Berlin and the Federal Republic of Germany will be facilitated and unimpeded. It will receive the most simple, expeditious and preferential treatment provided by international practice.

2   Accordingly,

(a) Conveyances sealed before departure may be used for the transport of civilian goods by road, rail and waterways between the Western Sectors of Berlin and the Federal Republic of Germany. Inspection procedures will be limited to the inspection of seals and accompanying documents.

(b) With regard to conveyances which cannot be sealed, such as open trucks, inspection procedures will be limited to the inspection of accompanying documents. In special cases where there is sufficient reason to suspect that unsealed conveyances contain either material intended for dissemination along the designated routes or persons or material put on board along these routes, the content of unsealed conveyances may be inspected. Procedures for dealing with such cases will be agreed by the competent German authorities.

(c) Through trains and buses may be used for travel between the Western Sectors of Berlin and the Federal Republic of Germany. Inspection procedures will not include any formalities other than identification of persons.

(d) Persons identified as through travellers using individual vehicles between the Western Sectors of Berlin and the Federal Republic of Germany on routes designated for through traffic will be able to proceed to their destinations without paying individual tolls and fees for the use of the transit routes. Procedures applied for such travellers shall not involve delay. The travellers, their vehicles and personal baggage will not be subject to search, detention or exclusion from use of the designated routes, except in special cases, as may be agreed by the competent German authorities, where there is sufficient reason to suspect that misuse of the transit routes is intended for purposes not related to direct travel to and from the Western Sectors of Berlin and contrary to generally applicable regulations concerning public order.

(e) Appropriate compensation for fees and tolls and for other costs related to traffic on the communication routes between the Western Sectors of Berlin and the Federal Republic of Germany, including the maintenance of adequate routes, facilities and installations used for such traffic, may be made in the form of an annual lump sum paid to the German Democratic Republic by the Federal Republic of Germany.

3   Arrangements implementing and supplementing the provisions of paragraphs 1 and 2 above will be agreed by the competent German authorities.

Annex II

Communication from the Governments of the French Republic, the United Kingdom and the United States of America to the Government of the Union of Soviet Socialist Republics

The Governments of the French Republic, the United Kingdom and the United States of America, with reference to Part II (B) of the Quadripartite Agreement of this date and after consultation with the Government of the Federal Republic of Germany, have the honor to inform the Government of the Union of Soviet Socialist Republics that:

1   They declare, in the exercise of their rights and responsibilities, that the ties between the Western Sectors of Berlin and the Federal Republic of Germany will be maintained and developed, taking into account that these Sectors continue not to be a constituent part of the Federal Republic of Germany and not to be governed by it. The provisions of the Basic Law of the Federal Republic of Germany and of the Constitution operative in the Western Sectors of Berlin which contradict the above have been suspended and continue not to be in effect.

2   The Federal President, the Federal Government, the Bundesversammlung, the Bundesrat and the Bundestag, including their Committees and Fraktionen, as well as other state bodies of the Federal Republic of Germany will not perform in the Western Sectors of Berlin constitutional or official acts which contradict the provisions of paragraph 1.

3   The Government of the Federal Republic of Germany will be represented in the Western Sectors of Berlin to the authorities of the three Governments and to the Senat by a permanent liaison agency.

Annex III

Communication from the Government of the Union of Soviet Socialist Repub-

lics to the Governments of the French Republic, the United Kingdom and the United States of America

The Government of the Union of Soviet Socialist Republics, with reference to Part II (C) of the Quadripartite Agreement of this date and after consultation and agreement with the Government of the German Democratic Republic, has the honor to inform the Governments of the French Republic, the United Kingdom and the United States of America that:

1   Communications between the Western Sectors of Berlin and areas bordering on these Sectors and those areas of the German Democratic Republic which do not border on these Sectors will be improved.

2   Permanent residents of the Western Sectors of Berlin will be able to travel to and visit such areas for compassionate, family, religious, cultural or commercial reasons, or as tourists, under conditions comparable to those applying to other persons entering these areas. In order to facilitate visits and travel, as described above, by permanent residents of the Western Sectors of Berlin, additional crossing points will be opened.

3   The problems of the small enclaves, including Steinstuecken, and of other small areas may be solved by exchange of territory.

4   Telephonic, telegraphic, transport and other external communications of the Western Sectors of Berlin will be expanded.

5   Arrangements implementing and supplementing the provisions of paragraphs 1 to 4 above will be agreed by the competent German authorities.

Annex IV

A   Communication from the Governments of the French Republic, the United Kingdom and the United States of America to the Government of the Union of Soviet Socialist Republics

The Governments of the French Republic, the United Kingdom and the United States of America, with reference to Part II (D) of the Quadripartite Agreement of this date and after consultation with the Government of the Federal Republic of Germany, have the honor to inform the Government of the Union of Soviet Socialist Republics that:

1   The Governments of the French Republic, the United Kingdom and the United States of America maintain their rights and responsibilities relating to the representation abroad of the interests of the Western Sectors of Berlin and their permanent residents, including those rights and responsibilities concerning matters of security and status, both in international organizations and in relations with other countries.

2   Without prejudice to the above and provided that matters of security and status are not affected, they have agreed that:

(a) The Federal Republic of Germany may perform consular services for permanent residents of the Western Sectors of Berlin.

(b) In accordance with established procedures, international agreements and arrangements entered into by the Federal Republic of Germany may be extended to the Western Sectors of Berlin provided that the extension of such agreements and arrangements is specified in each case.

(c) The Federal Republic of Germany may represent the interests of the Western Sectors of Berlin in international organizations and international conferences.

(d) Permanent residents of the Western Sectors of Berlin may participate jointly with participants from the Federal Republic of Germany in international exchanges and exhibitions. Meetings of international organizations and international conferences as well as exhibitions with international participation may be held in the Western Sectors of Berlin. Invitations will be issued by the Senat or jointly by the Federal Republic of Germany and the Senat.

3   The three Governments authorize the establishment of a Consulate General of the USSR in the Western Sectors of Berlin accredited to the appropriate authorities of the three Governments in accordance with the usual procedures applied in those Sectors, for the purpose of performing consular services, subject to provisions set forth in a separate document of this date.

B   Communication From the Government of the Union of Soviet Socialist Republics to the Governments of the French Republic, the United Kingdom and the United States of America

The Government of the Union of Soviet Socialist Republics, with reference to Part II (D) of the Quadripartite Agreement of this date and to the communication of the Governments of the French Republic, the United Kingdom and the United States of America with regard to the representation abroad of the interests of the Western Sectors of Berlin and their permanent residents, has the honor to inform the Governments of the French Republic, the United Kingdom and the United States of America that:

1   The Government of the Union of Soviet Socialist Republics takes note of the fact that the three Governments maintain their rights and responsibilities relating to the representation abroad of the interests of the Western Sectors of Berlin and their permanent residents, including those rights and responsibilities concerning matters of security and status, both in international organizations and in relations with other countries.

2   Provided that matters of security and status are not affected, for its part it will raise no objection to:

(a) the performance by the Federal Republic of Germany of consular services for permanent residents of the Western Sectors of Berlin;

(b) in accordance with established procedures, the extension to the Western Sectors of Berlin of international agreements and arrangements entered into by the Federal Republic of Germany provided that the extension of such agreements and arrangements is specified in each case;

(c) the representation of the interests of the Western Sectors of Berlin by the Federal Republic of Germany in international organizations and international conferences;

(d) the participation jointly with participants from the Federal Republic of Germany of permanent residents of the Western Sectors of Berlin in international exchanges and exhibitions, or the holding in those Sectors of meetings of international organizations and international conferences as well as exhibitions with international participation, taking into account that invitations will be issued by the Senat or jointly by the Federal Republic of Germany and the Senat.

3   The Government of the Union of Soviet Socialist Republics takes note of the fact that the three Governments have given their consent to the establishment of a Consulate General of the USSR in the Western Sectors of Berlin. It will be accredited to the appropriate authorities of the three Governments, for purposes and subject to provisions described in their communication and as set forth in a separate document of this date.

Agreed minute I

It is understood that permanent residents of the Western Sectors of Berlin shall, in order to receive at appropriate Soviet offices visas for entry into the Union of Soviet Socialist Republics, present:

(a) a passport stamped "Issued in accordance with the Quadripartite Agreement of September 3, 1971";

(b) an identity card or other appropriately drawn up document confirming that the person requesting the visa is a permanent resident of the Western Sectors of Berlin and containing the bearer's full address and a personal photograph.

During his stay in the Union of Soviet Socialist Republics, a permanent resident of the Western Sectors of Berlin who has received a visa in this way may carry both documents or either of them, as he chooses. The visa issued by a Soviet office will serve as the basis for entry into the Union of Soviet Socialist Republics, and the passport or identity card will serve as the basis for consular services in accordance with the Quadripartite Agreement during the stay of that person in the territory of the Union of Soviet Socialist Republics.

The above-mentioned stamp will appear in all passports used by permanent residents of the Western Sectors of Berlin for journeys to such countries as may require it.

Agreed minute II

Provision is hereby made for the establishment of a Consulate General of the

USSR in the Western Sectors of Berlin. It is understood that the details concerning this Consulate General will include the following. The Consulate General will be accredited to the appropriate authorities of the three Governments in accordance with the usual procedures applying in those Sectors. Applicable Allied and German legislation and regulations will apply to the Consulate General. The activities of the Consulate General will be of a consular character and will not include political functions or any matters related to quadripartite rights or responsibilities.

The three Governments are willing to authorize an increase in Soviet commercial activities in the Western Sectors of Berlin as described below. It is understood that pertinent Allied and German legislation and regulations will apply to these activities. This authorization will be extended indefinitely, subject to compliance with the provisions outlined herein. Adequate provision for consultation will be made. This increase will include establishment of an "Office of Soviet Foreign Trade Associations in the Western Sectors of Berlin", with commercial status, authorized to buy and sell on behalf of foreign trade associations of the Union of Soviet Socialist Republics. Soyuzpushnina, Prodintorg and Novoexport may each establish a bonded warehouse in the Western Sectors of Berlin to provide storage and display for their goods. The activities of the Intourist office in the British Sector of Berlin may be expanded to include the sale of tickets and vouchers for travel and tours in the Union of Soviet Socialist Republics and other countries. An office of Aeroflot may be established for the sale of passenger tickets and air freight services.

The assignment of personnel to the Consulate General and to permitted Soviet commercial organizations will be subject to agreement with the appropriate authorities of the three Governments. The number of such personnel will not exceed twenty Soviet nationals in the Consulate General; twenty in the office of the Soviet Foreign Trade Associations; one each in the bonded warehouses; six in the Intourist office; and five in the Aeroflot office. The personnel of the Consulate General and of permitted Soviet commercial organizations and their dependents may reside in the Western Sectors of Berlin upon individual authorization.

The property of the Union of Soviet Socialist Republics at Lietzenburgerstrasse 11 and at Am Sandwerder 1 may be used for purposes to be agreed between appropriate representatives of the three Governments and of the Government of the Union of Soviet Socialist Republics.

Details of implementation of the measures above and a time schedule for carrying them out will be agreed between the four Ambassadors in the period between the signature of the Quadripartite Agreement and the signature of the Final Quadripartite Protocol envisaged in that Agreement.

Exchange of notes

The Ambassadors of the French Republic, the United Kingdom of Great Britain and Northern Ireland and the United States of America have the honor, with reference to the statements contained in Annex II of the Quadripartite Agreement to be signed on this date concerning the relationship between the Federal Republic of Germany and the Western Sectors of Berlin, to inform the Ambassador of the Union of Soviet Socialist Republics of their intention to send to the Chancellor of the Federal Republic of Germany immediately following signature of the Quadripartite Agreement a letter containing clarifications and interpretations which represent the understanding of their Governments of the statements contained in Annex II of the Quadripartite Agreement. A copy of the letter to be sent to the Chancellor of the Federal Republic of Germany is attached to this Note.

The Ambassadors avail themselves of this opportunity to renew to the Ambassador of the Union of Soviet Socialist Republics the assurances of their highest consideration.

> *Jean Sauvagnargues*
> *Roger Jackling*
> *Kenneth Rush*

September 3, 1971.

ATTACHMENT TO THREE-POWER NOTE

His Excellency
The Chancellor of the
Federal Republic of Germany,
Bonn.

Your Excellency: With reference to the Quadripartite Agreement signed on September 3, 1971, our Governments wish by this letter to inform the Government of the Federal Republic of Germany of the following clarifications and interpretations of the statements contained in Annex II, which was the subject of consultation with the Government of the Federal Republic of Germany during the quadripartite negotiations.

These clarifications and interpretations represent the understanding of our Governments of this part of the Quadripartite Agreement, as follows:

a   The phrase in Paragraph 2 of Annex II of the Quadripartite Agreement which reads: "...will not perform in the Western Sectors of Berlin constitutional or official acts which contradict the provisions of Paragraph 1" shall be interpreted to mean acts in exercise of direct state authority over the Western Sectors of Berlin.

133

b Meetings of the Bundesversammlung will not take place and plenary sessions of the Bundesrat and the Bundestag will continue not to take place in the Western Sectors of Berlin. Single committees of the Bundesrat and the Bundestag may meet in the Western Sectors of Berlin in connection with maintaining and developing the ties between those Sectors and the Federal Republic of Germany. In the case of Fraktionen, meetings will not be held simultaneously.

c The liaison agency of the Federal Government in the Western Sectors of Berlin includes departments charged with liaison functions in their respective fields.

d Established procedures concerning the applicability to the Western Sectors of Berlin of legislation of the Federal Republic of Germany shall remain unchanged.

e The term "state bodies" in Paragraph 2 of Annex II shall be interpreted to mean: the Federal President, the Federal Chancellor, the Federal Cabinet, the Federal Ministers and Ministries, and the branch offices of those Ministries, the Bundesrat and the Bundestag, and all Federal courts.

Accept, Excellency, the renewed assurance of our highest esteem.

For the Government of the French Republic:

For the Government of the United Kingdom of Great Britain and Northern Ireland:

For the Government of the United States of America:

REPLY FROM THE AMBASSADOR OF THE U.S.S.R.

Translation

The Ambassador of the Union of Soviet Socialist Republics has the honor to acknowledge receipt of the note of the Ambassadors of the French Republic, the United Kingdom of Great Britain and Northern Ireland, and the United States of America, dated September 3, 1971, and takes cognizance of the communication of the three Ambassadors.

The Ambassador avails himself of this opportunity to renew to the Ambassadors of the French Republic, the United Kingdom, and the United States of America the assurance of his very high consideration.

Pyotr A. Abrasimov

September 3, 1971.

France-U.S.-U.K. Letter to the Chancellor of the Federal Republic of Germany

September 3, 1971.

His Excellency

The Chancellor of the
Federal Republic of Germany,
Bonn.

Your Excellency: We have the honor by means of this letter to convey to the Government of the Federal Republic of Germany the text of the Quadripartite Agreement signed this day in Berlin. The Quadripartite Agreement was concluded by the Four Powers in the exercise of their rights and responsibilities with respect to Berlin.

We note that, pursuant to the terms of the Agreement and of the Final Quadripartite Protocol which ultimately will bring it into force, the text of which has been agreed, these rights and responsibilities are not affected and remain unchanged. Our Governments will continue, as heretofore, to exercise supreme authority in the Western Sectors of Berlin, within the framework of the Four Power responsibility which we share for Berlin as a whole.

In accordance with Part II (A) of the Quadripartite Agreement, arrangements implementing and supplementing the provisions relating to civilian traffic will be agreed by the competent German authorities. Part III of the Quadripartite Agreement provides that the Agreement will enter into force on a date to be specified in a Final Quadripartite Protocol which will be concluded when the arrangements envisaged between the competent German authorities have been agreed. It is the request of our Governments that the envisaged negotiations now take place between authorities of the Federal Republic of Germany, also acting on behalf of the Senat, and authorities of the German Democratic Republic.

Part II (B) and (D) and Annexes II and IV of the Quadripartite Agreement relate to the relationship between the Western Sectors of Berlin and the Federal Republic. In this connection, the following are recalled inter alia:

the communications of the three Western Military Governors to the Parliamentary Council of 2 March, 22 April and 12 May, 1949,

the letter of the three High Commissioners to the Federal Chancellor concerning the exercise of the reserved Allied rights relating to Berlin of 26 May 1952 in the version of the letter X of 23 October 1954,

the Aide Memoire of the three Governments of 18 April 1967 concerning the decision of the Federal Constitutional Court of 20 January 1966 in the Niekisch case.

Our Governments take this occasion to state, in exercise of the rights and responsibilities relating to Berlin, which they retained in Article 2 of the Convention on Relations between the Three Powers and the Federal Republic of Germany of 26 May 1952 as amended October 23, 1954, that Part II (B) and (D) and Annexes II and IV of the Quadripartite Agreement concerning the relationship between the Federal Republic of Germany and the Western

Sectors of Berlin accord with the position in the above mentioned documents, which remains unchanged.

With regard to the existing ties between the Federal Republic and the Western Sectors of Berlin, it is the firm intention of our Governments that, as stated in Part II (B) (1) of the Quadripartite Agreement, these ties will be maintained and developed in accordance with the letter from the three High Commissioners to the Federal Chancellor on the exercise of the reserved rights relating to Berlin of 26 May 1952, in the version of letter X of October 23, 1954, and with pertinent decisions of the Allied Kommandatura of Berlin.

Accept, Excellency, the renewed assurance of our highest esteem.

For the Government of the French Republic:

Jean Sauvagnargues

For the Government of the United Kingdom of Great Britain and Northern Ireland:

Roger Jackling

For the Government of the United States of America:

Kenneth Rush

Communication From Allied Kommandatura to the Governing Mayor of Berlin

BKC/L (71)1 DATED SEPTEMBER 3

The Allied Kommandatura refers to the Quadripartite Agreement signed on September 3 in Berlin.

Part II (C) and Annex III, Paragraph 5, of the Quadripartite Agreement provide that arrangements implementing and supplementing the provisions relating to travel, communications and the exchange of territory will be agreed by the competent German authorities. Part IV of the Quadripartite Agreement provides that the Agreement will enter into force on a date to be specified in a Final Quadripartite Protocol which will be concluded when the arrangements envisaged between the competent German authorities have been agreed.

The Senat of Berlin is hereby authorized and requested to conduct appropriate negotiations on the subjects covered in Paragraphs 1, 2 and 3 in Annex III.

Draft Protocol on Entry into Force

FINAL QUADRIPARTITE PROTOCOL

The Governments of the United States of America, the French Republic, the

Union of Soviet Socialist Republics and the United Kingdom of Great Britain and Northern Ireland,

Having in mind Part II of the Quadripartite Agreement of September 3, 1971, and taking note with satisfaction of the fact that the agreements and arrangements mentioned below have been concluded,

Have agreed on the following:

1 The four Governments, by virtue of this Protocol bring into force the Quadripartite Agreement, which like this Protocol, does not affect quadripartite agreements or decisions previously concluded or reached.

2 The four Governments proceed on the basis that the agreements and arrangements concluded between the competent German authorities (list of agreements and arrangements) shall enter into force simultaneously with the Quadripartite Agreement.

3 The Quadripartite Agreement and the consequent agreements and arrangements of the competent German authorities referred to in this Protocol settle important issues examined in the course of the negotiations and shall remain in force together.

4 In the event of a difficulty in the application of the Quadripartite Agreement or any of the above mentioned agreements or arrangements which any of the four Governments considers serious, or in the event of non-implementation of any part thereof, that Government will have the right to draw the attention of the other three Governments to the provisions of the Quadripartite Agreement and this Protocol and to conduct the requisite quadripartite consultations in order to ensure the observance of the commitments undertaken and to bring the situation into conformity with the Quadripartite Agreement and this Protocol.

5 This Protocol enters into force on the date of signature.

Done at the building formerly occupied by the Allied Control Council in the American Sector of Berlin this .... day of .... 1971, in four originals, each in the English, French and Russian languages, all texts being equally authentic.

For the Government of the United States of America:

For the Government of the French Republic:

For the Government of the Union of Soviet Socialist Republics:

For the Government of the United Kingdom of Great Britain and Northern Ireland:

Source: The Department of State Bulletin, Vol. LXV, No. 1683, Sept. 27, 1971, pp. 218–325.

Appendix 4

Treaty on the basis of relations between the Federal Republic of Germany and the German Democratic Republic

The High Contracting Parties,
Conscious of their responsibility for the preservation of peace,
Anxious to render a contribution to détente and security in Europe,
Aware that the inviolability of frontiers and respect for the territorial integrity and sovereignty of all States in Europe within their present frontiers are a basic condition for peace,
Recognizing that therefore the two German States have to refrain from the threat or use of force in their relations,
Proceeding from the historical facts and without prejudice to the different views of the Federal Republic of Germany and the German Democratic Republic on fundamental questions, including the national question,
Desirous to create the conditions for co-operation between the Federal Republic of Germany and the German Democratic Republic for the benefit of the people in the two German States,
Have agreed as follows:

Article 1

The Federal Republic of Germany and the German Democratic Republic shall develop normal, good-neighbourly relations with each other on the basis of equal rights.

Article 2

The Federal Republic of Germany and the German Democratic Republic will be guided by the aims and principles laid down in the United Nations Charter, especially those of the sovereign equality of all States, respect for their independence, autonomy and territorial integrity, the right of self-determination, the protection of human rights, and non-discrimination.

Article 3

In conformity with the United Nations Charter the Federal Republic of Germany and the German Democratic Republic shall settle any disputes between them exclusively by peaceful means and refrain from the threat or use of force.

They reaffirm the inviolability now and in the future of the frontier existing between them and undertake fully to respect each other's territorial integrity.

Article 4

The Federal Republic of Germany and the German Democratic Republic proceed on the assumption that neither of the two States can represent the other in the international sphere or act on its behalf.

Article 5

The Federal Republic of Germany and the German Democratic Republic shall promote peaceful relations between the European States and contribute to security and co-operation in Europe.

They shall support efforts to reduce forces and arms in Europe without allowing disadvantages to arise for the security of those concerned.

The Federal Republic of Germany and the German Democratic Republic shall support, with the aim of general and complete disarmament under effective international control, efforts serving international security to achieve armaments limitation and disarmament, especially with regard to nuclear weapons and other weapons of mass destruction.

Article 6

The Federal Republic of Germany and the German Democratic Republic proceed on the principle that the sovereign jurisdiction of each of the two States is confined to its own territory. They respect each other's independence and autonomy in their internal and external affairs.

Article 7

The Federal Republic of Germany and the German Democratic Republic declare their readiness to regulate practical and humanitarian questions in the process of normalization of their relations. They shall conclude agreements with a view to developing and promoting on the basis of the present Treaty and for their mutual benefit co-operation in the fields of economics, science and technology, transport, judicial relations, posts and telecommunications, health, culture, sport, environmental protection, and in other fields. The details have been agreed in the Supplementary Protocol.

Article 8

The Federal Republic of Germany and the German Democratic Republic shall exchange Permanent Missions. They shall be established at the respective Government's seat.

Practical questions relating to the establishment of the Missions shall be dealt with separately.

Article 9

The Federal Republic of Germany and the German Democratic Republic agree that the present Treaty shall not affect the bilateral and multilateral international treaties and agreements already concluded by them or relating to them.

Article 10

The present Treaty shall be subject to ratification and shall enter into force on the day after the exchange of notes to that effect.

IN WITNESS WHEREOF the plenipotentiaries of the High Contracting Parties have signed this Treaty.

DONE at .... on .... 1972, in duplicate in the German language.

For the Federal Republic
of Germany

For the German
Democratic Republic

Source: The Bulletin, Press and Information Office of the Government of the Federal Republic of Germany (unofficial translation). no. 38/vol. 20, Bonn, November, 14, 1972.

Supplementary Protocol to the Treaty on the basis of relations between the Federal Republic of Germany and the German Democratic Republic

I

Re Article 3

The Federal Republic of Germany and the German Democratic Republic have agreed to form a Commission composed of agents of the Governments of the two States. They will review and, where necessary, renew or supplement the marking of the frontier existing between the two States and draw up the necessary documentation on the course of the frontier. In the same way the Commission will contribute to regulating other problems connected with the course of the frontier, e.g. water management, energy supply and the prevention of damage.

The Commission shall commence its work after the signing of the Treaty.

II

Re Article 7

1 Trade between the Federal Republic of Germany and the German

Democratic Republic shall be developed on the basis of the existing agreements.

The Federal Republic of Germany and the German Democratic Republic shall conclude long-term agreements with a view to promoting the continued development of their economic relations, adapting outdated arrangements, and improving the structure of trade.

2   The Federal Republic of Germany and the German Democratic Republic proclaim their intention to develop co-operation in the fields of science and technology for their mutual benefit and to conclude the necessary treaties for this purpose.

3   The co-operation in the field of traffic which began with the Treaty of 26 May 1972 shall be widened and intensified.

4   The Federal Republic of Germany and the German Democratic Republic declare their readiness to regulate their judicial relations as simply and expediently as possible by treaty in the interests of those seeking justice, especially in the fields of civil and criminal law.

5   The Federal Republic of Germany and the German Democratic Republic agree to conclude an agreement on posts and telecommunications on the basis of the Constitution of the Universal Postal Union and the International Telecommunication Convention. They will notify the Universal Postal Union (UPU) and the International Telecommunication Union (ITU) of the conclusion of that agreement.

The existing agreements and the procedures beneficial to both sides will be incorporated in that agreement.

6   The Federal Republic of Germany and the German Democratic Republic declare their interest in co-operation in the field of health. They agree that the appropriate treaty shall also regulate the exchange of medicaments as well as the treatment of patients in special clinics and sanatoria as far as practicable.

7   The Federal Republic of Germany and the German Democratic Republic intend to develop their cultural co-operation. To this end they shall enter into negotiations on the conclusion of intergovernmental agreements.

8   The Federal Republic of Germany and the German Democratic Republic reaffirm their preparedness to assist the appropriate sports organizations, after the Treaty has been signed, in bringing about arrangements for the promotion of relations in the field of sport.

9   Agreements are to be concluded between the Federal Republic of Germany and the German Democratic Republic in the field of environmental protection in order to help prevent hazards and harm to each other.

10   The Federal Republic of Germany and the German Democratic Republic will conduct negotiations with a view to enhancing the acquisition of each other's books, periodicals, radio and television productions.

11 The Federal Republic of Germany and the German Democratic Republic shall, in the interest of the people concerned, enter into negotiations to regulate non-commercial payment and clearing procedures. In this connexion they shall, in their mutual interest, give priority to the early conclusion of agreements on social grounds.

Protocol Note

Owing to the different legal positions with regard to questions of property and assets these matters could not be regulated by the Treaty.

Extension of agreements and arrangements to Berlin (West); representation of interests of Berlin (West)

Identical Statement by both Parties on signing the Treaty:

"It is agreed that the extension to Berlin (West) of agreements and arrangements envisaged in the Supplementary Protocol to Article 7 may be agreed in each individual case in conformity with the Quadripartite Agreement of 3 September 1971.

The Permanent Mission of the Federal Republic of Germany in the German Democratic Republic shall, in conformity with the Quadripartite Agreement of 3 September 1971, represent the interests of Berlin (West).

Arrangements between the German Democratic Republic and the Senate shall remain unaffected."

Political consultation

Identical Statement by both Parties on signing the Treaty:

"The two Governments have agreed to consult each other in the process of the normalization of relations between the Federal Republic of Germany and the German Democratic Republic on questions of mutual interest, in particular on those important for the safeguarding of peace in Europe."

Correspondence on an application for Membership in the United Nations

The Federal Chancellery
The State Secretary

Bonn,

To the
State Secretary to the
Council of Ministers of
the German Democratic Republic,

Dr. Michael Kohl

Berlin

Dear Herr Kohl,

I have the honour to inform you of the following:

The Government of the Federal Republic of Germany has noted that the Government of the German Democratic Republic initiates the necessary steps in conformity with domestic legislation to acquire membership of the United Nations Organization.

The two Governments will inform each other of the date on which the application will be made.

Yours faithfully,

(Signed: *Egon Bahr*)

State Secretary to the
Council of Ministers
of the German Democratic Republic

Berlin,

To the
State Secretary in the
Chancellery of the
Federal Republic of Germany,

Herr Egon Bahr,

Bonn

Dear Herr Bahr,

I have the honour to inform you of the following:

The Government of the German Democratic Republic has noted that the Government of the Federal Republic of Germany initiates the necessary steps in conformity with domestic legislation to acquire membership of the United Nations Organization.

The two Governments will inform each other of the date on which the application will be made.

Yours faithfully,

(Signed: *Dr. Michael Kohl*)

Correspondence with the text of the notes of the Federal Republic of Germany to the Three Powers and of the German Democratic Republic to the Soviet Union concerning Article 9 of the Treaty

The Federal Chancellery
The State Secretary

Bonn,

To the
State Secretary to the
Council of Ministers
of the German Democratic Republic,

Dr. Michael Kohl,

Berlin

Dear Herr Kohl,

I have the honour to inform you that the German Federal Foreign Office will today transmit in notes to the Ambassadors of the French Republic, the United Kingdom of Great Britain and Northern Ireland, and the United States of America to the Federal Republic of Germany the following text:

"The Federal Republic of Germany and the German Democratic Republic, with reference to Article 9 of the Treaty on the basis of relations, dated _____, affirm that rights and responsibilities of the Four Powers and the corresponding, related Quadripartite agreements, decisions and practices cannot be affected by this Treaty."

Yours faithfully,

(Signed: *Egon Bahr*)

State Secretary to the
Council of Ministers of
the German Democratic Republic

Berlin,

To the
State Secretary in the
Chancellery of the
Federal Republic of Germany,

Herr Egon Bahr,

Bonn

Dear Herr Bahr,

I have the honour to inform you that the Ministry of External Affairs will today transmit in a note to the Ambassador of the Union of Socialist Soviet Republics to the German Democratic Republic the following text:

"The German Democratic Republic and the Federal Republic of Germany, with reference to Article 9 of the Treaty on the basis of relations, dated ...., affirm that the rights and responsibilities of the Four Powers and the corresponding, related Quadripartite agreements, decisions and practices cannot be affected by this Treaty."

Yours faithfully,

(Signed: *Dr. Michael Kohl*)

Correspondence on the re-uniting of families, facilitation of travel, and improvements in non-commercial goods traffic

The State Secretary to
the Council of Ministers
of the German Democratic Republic

Berlin,

State Secretary in the
Federal Chancellery
of the Federal Republic of Germany,

Herr Egon Bahr,

Bonn

Dear Herr Bahr,

On the occasion of the signing today of the Treaty on the Basis of Relations between the German Democratic Republic and the Federal Republic of Germany, I have the honour to inform you of the following:

The Government of the German Democratic Republic will in the process of the normalization of relations and after the entry into force of the Treaty take steps to regulate matters in the following fields:

1 The solution of problems resulting from the separation of families.
2 Further to the exchange of letters of 26 May 1972, measures for the further improvement of border-crossing travel and visitor traffic, including tourism.
3 Improvement of non-commercial goods traffic between the German Democratic Republic and the Federal Republic of Germany:

146

– Further measures to facilitate border-crossing traffic in gift parcels and packages;
– further facilities for travellers to carry non-commercial goods in border-crossing travel and visitor traffic;
– corresponding review of existing import and export regulations;
– simplification of procedures to obtain permits for the removal of personal and household effects and for hereditaments.

Yours faithfully,

(Signed: Dr. *Michael Kohl*)

The Federal Chancellery
The State Secretary

Bonn,

To the
State Secretary to the
Council of Ministers
of the German Democratic Republic,

Dr. Michael Kohl,

Berlin

Dear Herr Kohl,

I have the honour to acknowledge receipt of your letter of today's date, which reads as follows:

"On the occasion of the signing today of the Treaty on the Basis of Relations between the German Democratic Republic and the Federal Republic of Germany, I have the honour to inform you of the following:

The Government of the German Democratic Republic will in the process of the normalization of relations and after the entry into force of the Treaty take steps to regulate matters in the following fields:

1 The solution of problems resulting from the separation of families.
2 Further to the exchange of letters of 26 May 1972, measures for the further improvement of border-crossing travel and visitor traffic, including tourism.
3 Improvement of non-commercial goods traffic between the German Democratic Republic and the Federal Republic of Germany:
– Further measures to facilitate border-crossing traffic in gift parcels and packages;

- further facilities for travellers to carry non-commercial goods in border-crossing travel and visitor traffic;
- corresponding review of existing import and export regulations;
- simplification of procedures to obtain permits for the removal of personal and household effects and for hereditaments."

Yours faithfully,

(Signed: *Egon Bahr*)

Correspondence on working possibilities for journalists

The Federal Chancellery
The State Secretary

Bonn,

To the
State Secretary to the
Council of Ministers
of the German Democratic Republic,

Dr. Michael Kohl,

Berlin

Dear Herr Kohl,

I have the honour, on behalf of the Government of the Federal Republic of Germany, to inform you of the following regarding the possibilities for journalists from the German Democratic Republic to work in the Federal Republic of Germany:

The Federal Republic of Germany shall within the framework of its applicable legislation accord journalists from the German Democratic Republic and their assistants the right to engage in their professional activities and freely to acquire and report information. It will enable journalists to carry on their activities as travelling correspondents and, on the basis of reciprocity, to take up residence and engage in their professional activities as permanent correspondents, in each case on condition that their professional activities remain within the limits of the law.

For permanent correspondents the following assurances are given:
- They will be entitled to the same treatment as correspondents from other states;
- They will be entitled, after their professional establishment, to enter and leave the country at any time using any of the customary means of transport;

- They will be able to work and move about freely in the Federal Republic of Germany and to communicate without delay news, opinions and commentaries;
- They will be allowed to use the news transmission media normally available to the public;
- They will be entitled to obtain any official information generally accessible to the public and the publishing media as well as information from the authorized persons and authorities;
- They will be entitled to carry with them equipment, materials and documents required for the personal exercise of their profession.

Journalists working as permanent correspondents of the German Democratic Republic in the Federal Republic of Germany will be required:
- to be accredited or established in accordance with the applicable modalities in the Federal Republic of Germany;
- to observe regulations and ordinances issued in the interest of security, crime prevention, protection of public health and of the rights and liberties of others.

Journalists within the meaning of this communication are persons who are regularly and professionally concerned as reporters, photographers, camera-men or technicians of the press, radio, television or of a news film company of the German Democratic Republic with obtaining, receiving or passing on information including opinions and commentaries for daily or periodical publications, press agencies, radio and television companies or news film companies of the German Democratic Republic.

Yours faithfully,

(Signed: *Egon Bahr*)

The State Secretary
to the Council of Ministers
of the German Democratic Republic

Berlin,

State Secretary in the
Federal Chancellery
of the Federal Republic of Germany,

Herr Egon Bahr,

Bonn

Dear Herr Bahr,

I have the honour, on behalf of the Government of the German Democratic Republic, to inform you of the following regarding the possibilities for journalists from the Federal Republic of Germany to work in the German Democratic Republic:

The German Democratic Republic shall within the framework of its applicable legislation accord journalists from the Federal Republic of Germany and their assistants the right to engage in their professional activities and freely to acquire and report information. It will enable journalists to carry on their activities as travelling correspondents and, on the basis of reciprocity, to take up residence and engage in their professional activities as permanent correspondents, in each case on condition that their professional activities remain within the limits of the law.

For permanent correspondents the following assurances are given:
– They will be entitled to the same treatment as correspondents from other states;
– They will be entitled, after their professional establishment, to enter and leave the country at any time using any of the customary means of transport;
– They will be able to work and move about freely in the German Democratic Republic and to communicate without delay news, opinions and commentaries;
– They will be allowed to use the news transmission media normally available to the public;
– They will be entitled to obtain any official information generally accessible to the public and the publishing media as well as information from the authorized persons and authorities;
– They will be entitled to carry with them the equipment, materials and documents required for the personal exercise of their profession.

Journalists working as permanent correspondents of the Federal Republic of Germany in the German Democratic Republic will be required:
– to be accredited or established with the applicable modalities in the German Democratic Republic;
– to observe regulations and ordinances issued in the interest of security, crime prevention, protection of public health and of the rights and liberties of others.

Journalists within the meaning of this communication are persons who are regularly and professionally concerned as reporters, photographers, cameramen or technicians of the press, radio, television or of a news film company of the Federal Republic of Germany with obtaining, receiving or passing on information including opinions and commentaries for daily or periodical publications, press agencies, radio and television companies or news film companies of the Federal Republic of Germany.

Yours faithfully,

(Signed: *Dr. Michael Kohl*)

Correspondence on the opening of four new border crossings

The State Secretary to
the Council of Ministers
of the German Democratic Republic

Berlin,

State Secretary in the
Federal Chancellery of
the Federal Republic of Germany,
Herr Egon Bahr,

Bonn

Dear Herr Bahr,

I have the honour to inform you of the following:

The German Democratic Republic will, at the time of the entry into force of the Treaty on the Basis of Relations, open the following road crossing points on the frontier with the Federal Republic of Germany for passenger traffic:

– Salzwedel
– Worbis
– Meiningen
– Eisfeld

Please convey this information to your Government

Yours faithfully,

(Signed: *Dr. Michael Kohl*)

The Federal Chancellery
The State Secretary

Bonn,

To the
State Secretary to the
Council of Ministers
of the German Democratic Republic,

Dr. Michael Kohl,

Berlin

Dear Herr Kohl,

With reference to your letters of ...., I have the honour to inform you of the following:

The Federal Republic of Germany will, at the time of the entry into force of the Treaty on the Basis of Relations, open the following crossing points for passenger traffic to correspond to the road frontier crossing points which you have communicated to me:

- Uelzen
- Duderstadt
- Bad Neustadt (Saale)
- Coburg

Yours faithfully,

(Signed: *Egon Bahr*)

Approval by the cabinet of results of the treaty negotiations

State Secretary Conrad Ahlers (Press and Information Office) announces that the Cabinet on November 7 approved the negotiation results with the GDR and has taken positive cognizance of the draft of the text for the Treaty on the Basis of the Relations between the Federal Republic of Germany and the German Democratic Republic as well as the accompanying documents.

State Secretary Egon Bahr (Chancellery) has been empowered to initial the treaty upon the proposal of the Federal Minister for Intra-German Relations. The initialing of the treaty will ensue shortly.

Correspondence on postal services and telecommunications

The State Secretary to the
Council of Ministers of the
German Democratic Republic

Berlin,

State Secretary in the
Chancellery of the
Federal Republic of Germany,

Herr Egon Bahr,

Bonn

Dear Herr Bahr,

I have the honour to inform you of the following:

The Government of the German Democratic Republic and the Government of the Federal Republic of Germany agree to enter into negotiations on a posts and telecommunications agreement after the initialling of the Treaty on the Basis of Relations between the German Democratic Republic and the Federal Republic of Germany. Until the conclusion of such an agreement the existing agreements and procedures shall continue to apply.

In view of the necessity of both States having equal membership of the Universal Postal Union (UPU) and the International Telecommunication Union (ITU), the Government of the German Democratic Republic wishes to inform the Government of the Federal Republic of Germany that the German Democratic Republic will, after the commencement of negotiations, take the necessary steps to obtain membership.

Yours faithfully,

(Signed: Dr. Michael Kohl)

The Federal Chancellery
The State Secretary

Bonn,

To the
State Secretary to the Council
of Ministers of the
German Democratic Republic,

Dr. Michael Kohl

Berlin,

Dear Herr Kohl,

I have the honour to inform you of the following:

The Government of the Federal Republic of Germany and the Govern-

153

ment of the German Democratic Republic agree to enter into negotiations on a posts and telecommunications agreement after the initialling of the Treaty on the Basis of Relations between the Federal Republic of Germany and the German Democratic Republic. Until the conclusion of such an agreement the existing agreements and procedures shall continue to apply.

In view of the necessity of both States having equal membership of the Universal Postal Union (UPU) and the International Telecommunication Union (ITU), the Government of the Federal Republic of Germany takes note of the fact that the German Democratic Republic will, after the commencement of negotiations, take the necessary steps to obtain membership.

Yours faithfully,

(Signed: *Egon Bahr*)

Index